Review

Roadmap
to 5th Grade
Reading:
VIRGINIA EDITION

by
Stephanie
Reents

Random House, Inc.
New York

www.review.com

This workbook was written by The Princeton Review, one of the nation's leaders in test preparation. The Princeton Review helps millions of students every year prepare for standardized assessments of all kinds. The Princeton Review offers the best way to help students excel on standardized tests.

The Princeton Review is not affiliated with Princeton University or Educational Testing Service.

Princeton Review Publishing, L.L.C.
160 Varick Street, 12th Floor
New York, NY 10013

E-mail: comments@review.com

Published in the United States by Random House, Inc., New York.

ISBN 0-375-75600-0

Editor: Russell Kahn
Director of Production: Iam Williams
Design Director: Tina McMaster
Development Editor: Rachael Nevins
Art Director: Neil McMahon
Production Manager: Mike Rockwitz
Production Editor: Lisbeth Dyer
Ollie the Ostrich illustrated by Paulo De Freitas Jr.
Manufactured in the United States of America

9 8 7 6 5 4

First Edition

ACKNOWLEDGMENTS

I want to thank Russell Kahn, my incredibly patient and dedicated editor, for making this book happen. Thanks also to the enormously talented production staff at the Princeton Review, including Robert Kurilla, Neil McMahon, and Lisbeth Dyer.

CONTENTS

Parent/Teacher Introduction

About This Book

The Princeton Review is one of the nation's leaders in test preparation. We prepare more than 2 million students every year with our courses, books, on-line services, and software programs. In addition to helping Virginia students with their Standards of Learning (SOL) Assessments, we coach students around the country on many other statewide standardized tests, as well as on college-entrance exams such as the SAT-I, SAT-II, PSAT, and ACT. Our strategies and techniques are unique and, most importantly, successful. Our goal is to reinforce skills that students have been taught in the classroom and to show them how to apply those skills to the specific format and structure of the Virginia SOL Grade 5 English: Reading/Literature and Research Assessment.

Roadmap to 5th Grade Reading: Virginia Edition contains three basic elements: lessons, test-preparation, and practice tests. Each lesson (or "mile") focuses on a specific skill, such as finding the main idea and supporting details of a passage. The miles walk students through the basics in ways that emphasize active learning and boil down information into easily retained and recalled chunks. Each lesson is coupled with focused test-prep that encourages students to apply what they've learned in exercises. The book also contains two full-length practice tests. Each practice test is modeled after the actual Virginia SOL Grade 5 Reading/Literature and Research Assessment in both style and content. This will help you assess which skills students should review and improve on before they take the actual SOL. It will also show you how much the students have improved after working on the lessons in this book. (Answer keys and explanations for the lessons and both practice tests are available beginning on page 171.)

We've also provided a Progress Chart as a way to encourage and motivate students. The Progress Chart is broken up into twenty-three miles, along with seven review sections called map checks. It will help students see how far they've come in their preparation. Studying for any test can be difficult for young students, and it is as important to encourage good study habits as it is to remediate students' weaknesses. Be vigilant about reminding students how well they are doing and how much they've learned. Building confidence goes a long way toward helping students succeed on any standardized test.

Before students begin their test preparation, take a moment to review the table of contents and to flip through the lessons in the book. We've tried to present the material in such a way that each skill presented builds on the previous one, but we realize that every student, and every class, has different strengths and weaknesses. There's no harm in students working on the lessons out of sequence.

ABOUT THE VIRGINIA SOL GRADE 5 READING/LITERATURE AND RESEARCH ASSESSMENT

All fifth-grade students in Virginia are required to take the Virginia Standards of Learning (SOL) Reading/Literature Assessment. The test contains a reading and a writing section. This book focuses on the reading portion of the test.

The reading test includes fifty-two multiple-choice questions. Ten of these questions will be field-test items that will not count toward students' scores. Because there is no way to differentiate the field-tested items from the scored items, students should answer all of the questions as if they count toward their scores. Students must choose one of four answer choices for each question. For each answer choice they select, they must fill in the corresponding bubble on the separate answer sheet provided.

Students' test scores are reported as either failing, proficient, or advanced. Students' SOL test scores in grades K–8 will be used as one factor in determining grade promotion or retention. Fifth-grade SOL scores may determine a student's track in middle school. By 2007 schools risk losing their accreditation if less than 70 percent of their students pass the SOL exams.

Note: Check with the Virginia Department of Education for the most recent information about score reporting. Check with your school district for the test's administration date in your area.

The Virginia Department of Education Web site has updates about the Virginia Standards of Learning:

http://www.pen.k12.va.us/VDOE/Instruction/sol.html

The Virginia Grade 5 SOL Reading/Literature and Research Assessment blueprints, which include a list of the standards assessed on the test, can also be found at the Virginia Department of Education Web site:

http://www.pen.k12.va.us/VDOE/Assessment/soltests/read5.html

PRACTICAL NOTES FOR TESTING DAY

- Because there is no guessing penalty, students should answer all of the questions on the test. They should not leave questions unanswered because they find them difficult. (Students should review the test-taking technique Getting Rid of Wrong Answer Choices on page 26 to improve their chances of correctly answering difficult questions.)

- The test is *untimed,* so students should not get anxious about finishing as quickly as possible. Remind students that they'll have as much time as they need.

NINE SIMPLE THINGS YOU CAN DO TO HELP STUDENTS READ BETTER

1. **Read to your students.**

   Read stories aloud to your students and then discuss the stories with them. Talk together about the characters and discuss what happens in the story, especially if the plot turns out to be surprising. You may want to have students read along with you, or ask them to locate words on the page.

2. **Help your students read on their own.**

   Independent reading helps students to succeed in school. Help your students get their own library cards and let them pick out their own books. Suggest reading as a fun free-time activity.

3. **Show your students why reading is important.**

   Explain to your students how reading plays a vital role in everyday life. Show how strong reading skills can help them with both practical (in driving, following directions, and reading receipts, bills, and contracts) and entertaining (reading newspapers, magazines, and books) aspects of life. Make sure your students set aside time during the day to read.

4. **Make sure students have writing tools available.**

   Students generally want to learn how to read and write. Help them to do that by having paper, pencils, pens, or crayons available for them at all times. Work with them if they ask you to.

5. **Set a good example.**

   Students learn from their parents and teachers. You can set a good example for them by reading newspapers, magazines, and books.

6. **Supply books on tape for learning disabled students.**

   Learning disabilities may frustrate young readers. Books on tape can be a terrific substitute for reading for learning disabled readers. If you can't find books on tape for your students' favorite books, you can always record them yourself.

7. **Track students' progress.**

   Create a system for students so that they can visualize their progress. It helps students to build confidence if they can see how they are improving their skills. The Progress Chart on pages 8–9 is a great way to show students' development in this book.

8. **Ask students to tell you about events in their lives.**

   Describing the events and telling the stories that occur in their lives helps students learn about stories in general. It can also help them understand what the stories they read mean.

9. **Use television as a tool.**

   Educational television programs have the power to teach students about many subjects. Try to restrict the use of noneducational television.

STUDENT INTRODUCTION

ABOUT THIS BOOK

We're guessing that you don't like tests. Given the choice, you'd never take another test again, right? Well, the *Roadmap to 5th Grade Reading: Virginia Edition* makes it fun to learn how to take tests. The book includes games to play, puzzles to finish, maps to fill in, and questions to answer.

Every lesson in this book is another "mile" on a trip that ends with you doing your best on the Standards of Learning (SOL) Reading/Literature and Research test. Each mile reviews a skill that you'll be tested on. We'll take you step-by-step through all the basics. And after you review, you get a chance to show what you know. What could be more fun than that? Track yourself on the Progress Chart in the beginning of the book by coloring in every mile after you've finished it.

In no time flat, you'll be an expert at Virginia reading. The only thing left will be to show your parents and teachers what you've learned by acing your SOL test. And just in case you're worried about how well you do, we've given you two complete practice tests. These practice tests can show you exactly how great your reading skills are!

You still might not like tests. That's okay. But by the time you get to the end of the *Roadmap to 5th Grade Reading,* you'll be ready to do your best on them!

WHAT ELSE CAN I DO?

There are other things you can do to prepare for the Virginia SOL Reading/Literature and Research test. You should:

- **Ask questions.** If you are confused after you finish a mile (or even just one question), ask a parent or teacher for help. Asking questions is the best way to make sure you understand what you have to do to do your best!

- **Read.** Read everything you can. Read the newspaper, magazines, books, plays, poems, comics, the back of your cereal box. The more you read the better you read. And the better you read the more likely you are to do well on the SOL reading test.

- **Learn new words.** Vocabulary is a big part of this test. The more words you know the easier the test will seem. Try carrying index cards with you. Any time you come across a word you don't know, write it down. When you have time, look up the definition and write it on the back of the card. You can turn learning vocabulary into a game. Use your cards to test yourself. Set goals for learning new words every week. Ask teachers for help if you want. I bet they can suggest some great new words to learn.

- **Play games.** Word games like Scrabble™, crossword puzzles, and even Mad Libs™ can improve your vocabulary.

- **Eat well and get a good night's sleep.** Your brain is part of your body. Your body doesn't work well when you don't eat good food and get enough sleep. Neither does your brain. On the night before the test, make sure you go to bed at your normal time. You should also have a healthy breakfast on the morning of the testing day. Nothing will help you do better than being awake and alert while your taking your SOL Reading/Literature and Research test.

This is just the beginning of the road. There are great things to learn ahead. So buckle your seatbelt and get ready to take off down the first mile to Virginia Reading excellence.

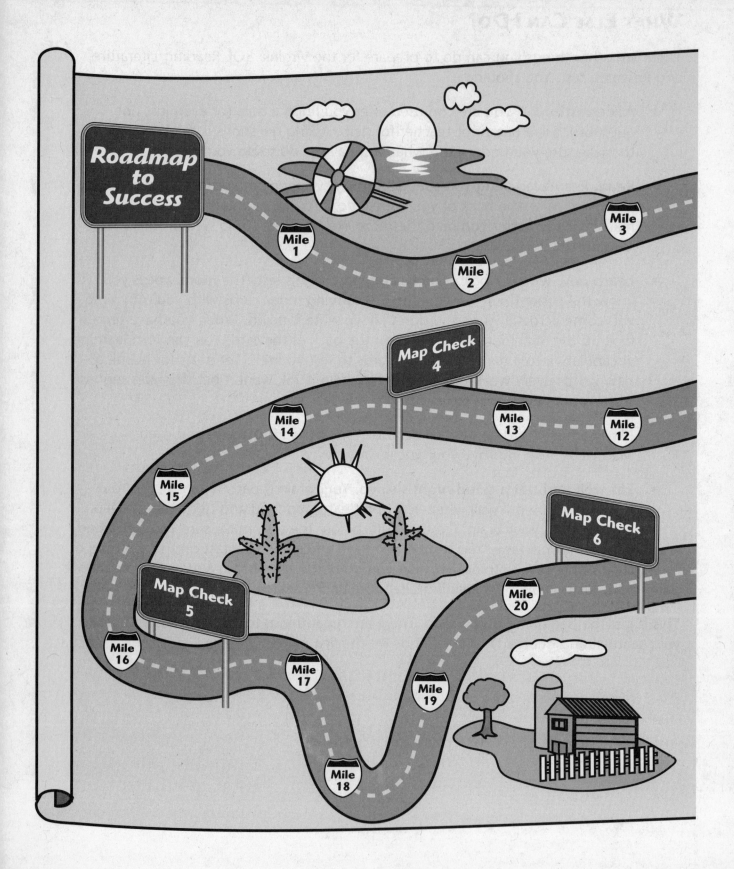

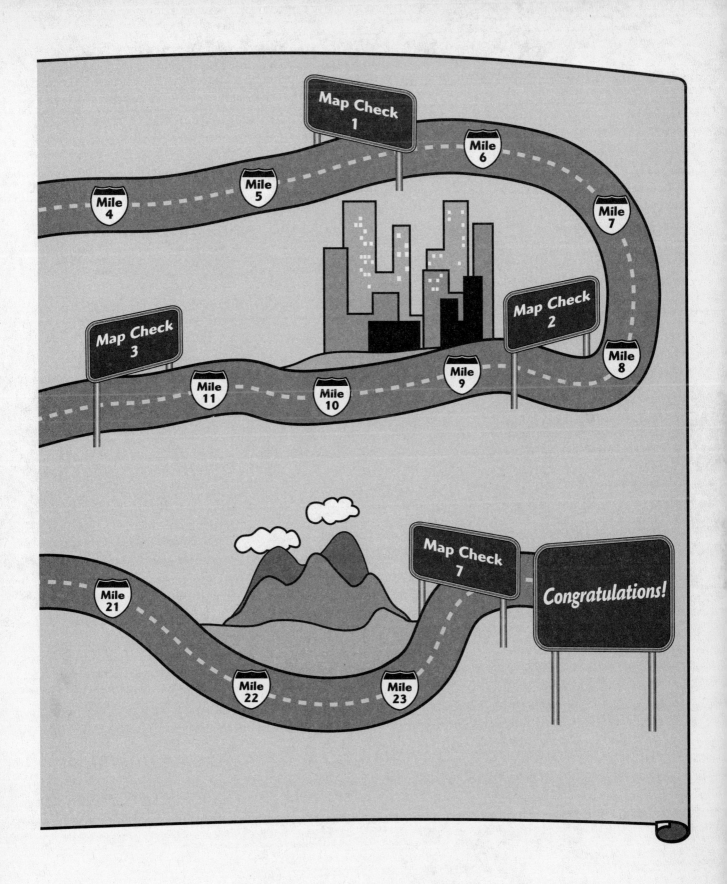

MILE-BY-MILE

Before setting off on an adventure, you usually consult a map. A map helps you figure out where you are going and how you're going to get there. Just like using a map for traveling, before you begin to read a book, you can look at its cover, read its title, and scan its pages to find out about the book and its contents. Predicting a book's subject matter will make reading it easier—because you'll know where you're headed.

Directions: Look at the book covers below. Based on the titles, write down what kinds of information or stories you would expect to read in each book. One example has been done for you.

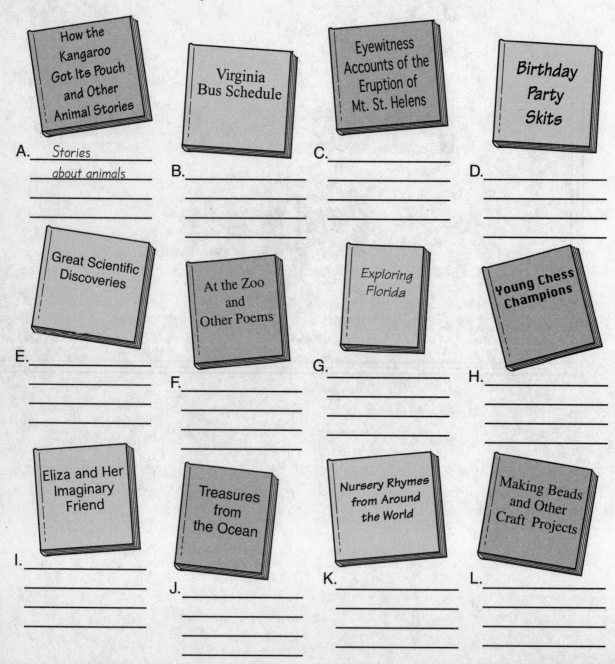

How the Kangaroo Got Its Pouch and Other Animal Stories

A. _Stories_
   about animals

Virginia Bus Schedule

B. _____

Eyewitness Accounts of the Eruption of Mt. St. Helens

C. _____

Birthday Party Skits

D. _____

Great Scientific Discoveries

E. _____

At the Zoo and Other Poems

F. _____

Exploring Florida

G. _____

Young Chess Champions

H. _____

Eliza and Her Imaginary Friend

I. _____

Treasures from the Ocean

J. _____

Nursery Rhymes from Around the World

K. _____

Making Beads and Other Craft Projects

L. _____

Read the titles of the two books that appear below. One book is fiction, and the other book is nonfiction. Identify the books by writing "Fiction" or "Nonfiction" next to the books. Then read the sentences below the books. Some sentences came from the fiction book, and some came from the nonfiction book. On the line next to each sentence, write "Fiction" or "Nonfiction."

 _____

 _____

1. One kind of fish called shad has 769 bones. _____

2. Fish can swallow people if they get angry. _____

3. Eric the Elephant can play songs with his trunk. _____

4. A black bear carried off a small child and raised him as a cub. _____

5. A snail can lay up to eighty-five eggs at a time. _____

6. Cats from Prussia can live to be one hundred years old. _____

7. The Komodo dragon is the world's largest lizard. _____

8. Elephants are born with large ears so they can fly. _____

9. Porcupine quills are about 7.5 centimeters long. _____

10. A pack of laughing hyenas took over half of Newport News. _____

Write one more statement that you would expect to find in *Amazing Animal Facts*.

11. _____

Write one more statement that you might find in *Fantastic Animal Stories*.

12. _____

A **historical fiction** story is a made-up story that is set in the past but is based on true historical facts. For example, the story of Robin Hood is fictional because there was no real Robin Hood, but the story is historical fiction because it includes real people and places from the past. A **nonfiction** story is a true story. It describes events that actually happened to real people. It contains facts.

Directions: The box below lists the names of five historical fiction and nonfiction stories. Read each passage, and choose the best title from the box for it. Then answer whether each passage is historical fiction or nonfiction.

Abraham Lincoln's Beard	Frontier Diary
The American Revolution	Across the Ocean
Champions of Women's Rights	

From early in her life, Susan B. Anthony fought for equal treatment for women. Anthony was fired from her first job as a teacher when she complained that male teachers earned five times as much money as she did. After that, she moved on to bigger causes that affected many women.

13. **What is the best title for this passage?**

_____

14. **Is this passage historical fiction or nonfiction?**

_____

Mary angrily scribbled in her diary by the light of the kerosene lantern. She was upset. Her father had taken the wagon to city to buy supplies for the winter. As a result, Mary had to stay home instead of going to school. She loved school, even though the one-room schoolhouse was often freezing and had only a few books.

15. **What is the best title for this passage?**

_____

16. **Is this passage historical fiction or nonfiction?**

_____

Sometimes at night, when the master was far away in the big plantation house and the cotton had been picked, Sadie's grandmother would tell stories about the homeland across the ocean. "You can't even imagine what it was like," Sadie's grandmother said. "The forests were deep, dark, and endless. And they were full of wild creatures. Elephants were bigger than this house." Sadie's eyes grew large. She loved it when her grandmother told her about her home before this one.

17. What is the best title for this story?

_____

18. Is this passage historical fiction or nonfiction?

_____

On the eve of December 16, 1773, the men staged a bold protest. Disguised as Mohawk Indians, they jumped aboard the three ships anchored in the Boston harbor, seized the tea, and threw it overboard into the ocean. They were protesting the British government's decision to let the East India Company sell tea directly in the colonies. Although tea would sell at lower prices, these men and many others were angry. They were angry that Britain had once again made a decision without consulting the people whom it affected—the colonists.

19. What is the best title for this passage?

_____

20. Is this passage historical fiction or nonfiction?

_____

Grace Bedell, a young girl who lived in New York, wrote Abraham Lincoln a letter on Oct. 15, 1860. She gave the president-to-be some important advice: Grow a beard. "All the ladies like whiskers," the eleven-year-old wrote, "and they would tease their husbands to vote for you, and then you would be President." Lincoln acted on her advice. By February of 1861, he was fully bearded.

21. What is the best title for this passage?

_____

22. Is this passage historical fiction or nonfiction?

_____

MILE 2: WHY DO PEOPLE READ?

People read for many different purposes. There are probably three major purposes for which a person would read something.

- People read to have fun.

- People read to gain knowledge.

- People read to learn how to do things.

Directions: Look at the different types of subjects below. Each example shows a different type of writing. On the next page are the three different purposes for which people read. Write the name of each kind of reading selection under the column that best describes why someone would read it. Cross out the book after you have written your answer. You should do this to make sure you don't write the same book twice. The first example has been done for you.

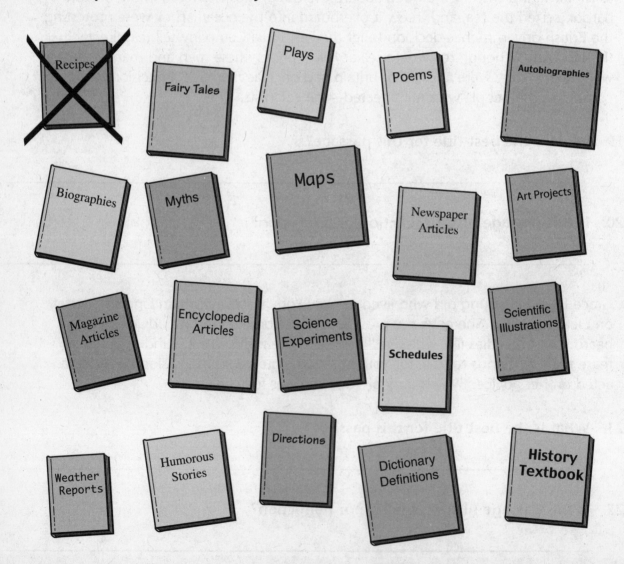

Keep in mind that the answers aren't set in stone. For example, people read newspapers primarily to gain information, but they also may read them to have fun. There are many right answers.

To have fun	To gain knowledge	To learn how to do things
		Recipes

Directions: The words in the box below list five different types of reading selections. Over the next two pages, read each of the short selections. Use the words from the box to complete the sentences that follow each selection. Then answer the question.

Poem   Schedule

Encyclopedia article   History book

Story

Mohandas Gandhi taught people to use a peaceful approach to change things they didn't like about the world. He began developing his philosophy during the years that he lived in South Africa. There, he realized that Indians did not have the same rights as white South African citizens. Gandhi began working to help Indians gain equal rights. Although he was arrested many times, he never used violence in his protests.

1. This reading selection is from _____

2. Why would somebody read this selection? _____

_____

_____

Richmond to Washington, D.C.

Bus #	Depart	Arrive
125	6:00 A.M.	8:00 A.M.
150	9:00 A.M.	11:00 A.M.
175	12:00 P.M.	2:00 P.M.
200	3:30 P.M.	5:30 P.M.
225	8:15 P.M.	10:15 P.M.

3. This reading selection is from _____.

4. Why would somebody read this selection? _____

_____

_____

Canada is the second largest country in the world, covering almost 4,000,000 square miles of land. Only Russia is larger. Canada has ten provinces and three territories, and its capital is Ottawa. The most populated city is Toronto, with well over 2,000,000 inhabitants. The estimated 31,000,000 residents of Canada mostly speak English and French—the country's official languages.

5.   This reading selection is from _____.

6.   Why would somebody read this selection? _____

_____

   It rained and rained and rained some more

   We were so scared to go outside

   Water filled the streets and lawns

   The puddles were as big as ponds

   It rained all night and it rained all morning

   It was a never-ending storm

   It rained at lunch and supper too

   It rained so much, there was nothing to do.

7.   This reading selection is from _____.

8.   Why would somebody read this selection? _____

_____

Min heard the door open, then the sound of someone tiptoeing downstairs. An owl called out, and Min shivered underneath her covers. It had been a strange day, beginning with the bottle she'd found on the beach. Tucked inside was a note written in an unknown language; something about the way it was written— with shaky handwriting in red ink—told Min that the message was important.

9.   This reading selection is from _____.

10.   Why would somebody read this selection?_____

_____

MILE 3: FINDING THE MAIN IDEA

The last time you returned from a vacation, your friends may have asked you, "What did you do on your trip?" Instead of telling them about every little thing, you probably told them about the main events of your vacation. Well, some questions may ask you to identify the main idea of a selection. Your job will be to figure out what the selection was mainly about.

In nonfiction passages, the main idea often comes in the first paragraph, and it describes the overall ideas presented in the article. For fiction passages, the main idea is usually what the main character (or you) learned from the story.

Directions: Read the four passages over the next two pages. After each one, answer the questions that follow.

Dom woke to the sound of rustling outside his bedroom door. He looked at the clock. It was 11:15 A.M. He jumped out of bed and rushed into the kitchen.

His sister was putting away the waffle iron. "Hi, sleepyhead," she said.

Dom gulped, "Are there any more waffles?"

"No," his sister replied. "We finished breakfast an hour ago."

Dom's stomach rumbled, and a frown spread across his face. His sister must have noticed his expression. "I guess you'll have to have cold cereal for breakfast," she said.

As Dom poured a bowl of cornflakes, he vowed to get up extra early the next day.

1.   What is the main idea of this passage? _____

_____

There are several different reasons that oceans are salty and rivers are not. As rivers travel to oceans, they collect salt and minerals from the bottom of the riverbeds. Rivers don't taste salty, however, because they are constantly receiving freshwater from sources like rain and natural springs.

In contrast, oceans fill with river water. This water is filled with all of the salt and minerals collected by the rivers. In addition, the ocean floor also contains minerals that dissolve in the water. Both of these make oceans salty.

2.   What is the main idea of this passage? _____

_____

Juanita was daydreaming about the new rollerblades she had received that morning for her birthday when she suddenly noticed her class was lining up.

"What's going on?" she whispered to her friend Susan.

"There's a special assembly," Susan replied with a mysterious smile. "Didn't you hear what Ms. Hornsby said?"

Juanita felt confused. "Juanita," Ms. Hornsby said. "I need to talk to you in the hallway." Juanita was sure she was in hot water with Ms. Hornsby.

"No daydreaming!" Ms. Hornsby said with a scowl on her face. Juanita walked into library with her head hung low.

"Surprise!" her friends shouted. "Happy birthday!"

Ms. Hornsby smiled at Juanita.

3.   What is the main idea of this passage? _____

_____

4.   What would be a good title for this passage? _____

_____

Dehydration is a common problem. When you're dehydrated it means that your body has lost or used more fluids than it has taken in. You lose fluids in lots of ordinary ways—by sweating, by going to the bathroom, and even by breathing.

There are many different ways our bodies tell us they need more fluids. Being thirsty is one sign. Feeling very tired even though you are getting a lot of sleep is another. Only going to the bathroom once or twice a day is another indication that you're dehydrated.

Because our bodies need water to stay healthy, pay attention to these signs and pour yourself a big glass of water.

5.   What is the main idea of this passage? _____

_____

6.   What would be a good title for this passage? _____

_____

Frederick Douglass

1   The famous author and champion of the rights of African Americans and women traveled a long way from his humble beginnings. Frederick Douglass was born in Tuckahoe, Maryland, in 1817 or 1818. He didn't know his exact birthday or even how old he was. He never met his father, although he knew that his father was a white man, and he was separated from his mother when he was just seven years old. As a slave, Douglass had few rights.

2   Life was difficult for slaves. Their masters made them work hard and gave them little in return. Each month, a slave usually received a small amount of food: eight pounds of pork or fish and one bushel of cornmeal. Each year, their masters gave them two shirts, a pair of pants, a pair of stockings, and one pair of shoes. Children who were slaves received even less.

3   Douglass began working when he was just a small boy. Because he was too young to work in the fields, he did odd jobs around his master's house. Before Douglass was nine years old, his master sent him to Baltimore to work for some relatives.

4   This was a turning point for him. The wife of his new master, Mrs. Auld, liked the young boy and began teaching him to read. However, when her husband found out about the lessons, he put a stop to them. It was against state law to teach him how to read! Douglass, however, was determined to learn more. He befriended some white boys who taught him what they were learning in school. As Douglass became more educated, he realized he was a slave, which meant he would be enslaved for life. Knowing this, he continued to study, with the goal of finding a way to gain his freedom.

5   Douglass began plotting ways to escape slavery. He saved the pennies that his master gave him, and finally, in 1838, he escaped to New York, a free state where slavery was illegal. Douglass was terrified that he would be caught and returned to his master. He worked hard, setting aside his earnings. Eventually, he saved $700. He used this money to pay his master and buy his freedom.

6   Having gained his freedom, Douglass used his gift for writing to persuade others to abolish slavery. He wrote three autobiographies about his struggles to escape his fate as a slave. He also published and edited a newspaper called *The North Star*, which called for the end of slavery.

7   Frederick Douglass's books and speeches in the 1800s helped support the African Americans' rights movement. After the Civil War, Congress passed the Fourteenth Amendment to the Constitution ensuring some guaranteed rights for African Americans. Douglass also helped convince voters to vote for Ulysses S. Grant in the 1868 presidential election. With Grant's victory, the Fifteenth Amendment was passed, allowing all citizens the right to vote, regardless of race.

7. Write a short summary of the selection about Frederick Douglass. Your summary should include only the most important ideas about Douglass.

_____

_____

_____

_____

_____

_____

8. Write down the main idea of the entire selection below.

_____

_____

_____

_____

Mile 4: Finding Supporting Ideas

Now that you've practiced finding the main idea, learn how to find supporting ideas. Supporting ideas help you draw a conclusion. Pretend you wake up one morning and look out the window. The sky is clear. Birds are chirping. The sun is shining brightly. You'd probably say to yourself, "It's going to be a beautiful day." You'd draw this conclusion based on the things (the sky, the birds, the sun) that you observed. These are supporting details.

Directions: Read the following story. On the page that follows, write the main idea of the story in the central circle of the diagram. Write the supporting ideas that support the story's main idea in the squares around the circle.

Kayaking

1   Last weekend, I went on a three-day kayaking trip led by two guides through the San Juan Islands. Kayaking is a very challenging activity.

2   We started our adventure at Andrews Bay on the west side of San Juan Island. First, we had to carry the kayaks to the edge of the beach. They were very heavy to carry. They got even heavier after we loaded them up with food and camping gear.

3   Packing them was difficult because all of our supplies and equipment had to fit into small storage bins in the front and back of the kayak. While I was trying to stuff my sleeping bag, tent, and dry bag (a waterproof bag that kept my clothes dry) into the front storage bin, I bruised my thumb. Ow!

4   After the guides gave us a quick lesson on paddling, we climbed into the boats. We were all wearing kayaking skirts that looked like rubber overalls with skirts. We attached the bottom of the skirts to a lip around the kayak opening in which we sat. This kept water from splashing into the kayaks. I had trouble attaching my kayaking skirt, but the guide came and helped me.

5   Kayaks are steered using rudders. The person sitting in the back controls the rudder with two foot pedals. Pushing on the pedals makes the kayak go left or right. It takes a while to get the hang of steering. For the first mile or two, we zigzagged back and forth. This, of course, made our journey longer and more tiring.

6   I thought kayaking would be easy because I have canoed a lot. Boy, was I wrong! Canoe paddles have a blade on one end; kayak paddles have blades on both ends. Kayaking is like pedaling a bike with your arms. You push the left blade into the water, then the right blade. The guides told us that it was important to push the paddle, rather than pull it. I guess I was doing it incorrectly, because my neck and arms got sore.

7   Once I finally started paddling correctly, we came to one of the most difficult parts of the trip: crossing Spieden Channel. Although the currents were flowing with us, the wind was blowing against us. It took us two hours to paddle six miles. Our kayak rocked up and down in the waves. Several times I ended up with a mouthful of seawater!

You can't imagine how happy I was when we paddled toward the campground on Stuart Island. But after drinking my first cup of hot chocolate, I started growing excited about the next day's kayaking challenges.

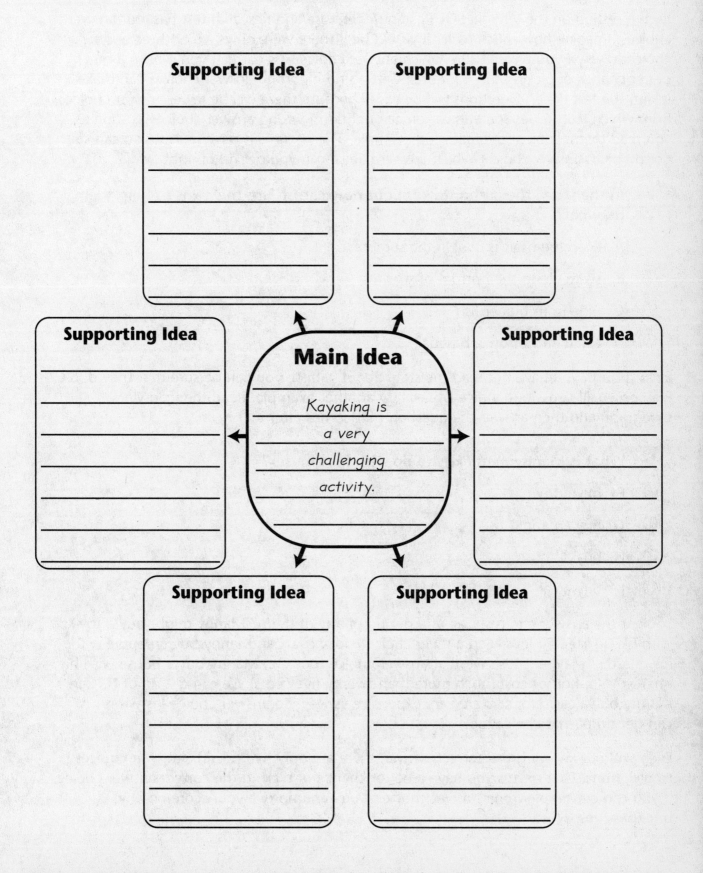

Supporting Idea

Supporting Idea

Supporting Idea

Main Idea

Kayaking is a very challenging activity.

Supporting Idea

Supporting Idea

Supporting Idea

MILE 5: ANSWERING MULTIPLE-CHOICE QUESTIONS

Each question on the Virginia SOL Reading/Literature and Research test has four answer choices. Imagine how much easier it would be if there were only two or three answer choices. Even if you weren't sure which answer choice was correct, you'd have a much better chance of picking the right one. Getting rid of wrong answer choices can make taking the test easier. Questions will be easier because there will be fewer answer choices from which to choose. Sometimes you can get rid of wrong answer choices as soon as you read them. Look at the following example. The passage is missing, but you can still get rid of an answer choice. Which answer choice can you get rid of right away?

▶ **In the story, the author talks about how catfish use their fins to help them do what?**

○ **A** keep themselves cool in the summer

○ **B** swim along the bottom of streams

○ **C** hide from bigger fish

○ **D** catch and throw a baseball

Even though you have not read the story about catfish, you can be sure that they don't play baseball! Cross out choice **D**. Let's try another example. Read the following paragraph and then answer the question that comes after it.

▶ **What is Manny *most likely* to do with his quarter?**

○ **F** buy a toy

○ **G** buy an apple

○ **H** buy a house

○ **J** buy a car

Look at the answer choices. Can you get rid of any of them? Manny might buy a toy with his quarter. So let's keep answer choice **F** for now. Can Manny buy an apple with his quarter? Maybe. Let's save that answer choice too. Can Manny buy a house with his quarter? No, houses cost much more than twenty-five cents! We can get rid of **H**. Can Manny buy a car? No, cars are very expensive as well. So answer choice **J** is wrong. We can get rid of that choice too.

Even without knowing the correct answer, there are only two possible answer choices to pick from. That means you have a better chance of picking the correct answer choice. If you can get rid of wrong answer choices, you can improve your score on any multiple-choice test!

Directions: Now it's your turn to practice getting rid of wrong answer choices. Read the following paragraph and then answer the questions that follow it. As you answer the questions, get rid of as may wrong answer choices as you can.

Drew and Cindy were late for school again. As usual, it was Drew's fault. The alarm clock was in Drew's room, and he slept through the alarm at least three times a week. Cindy would get ready as fast as she could, but it was usually too late. Cindy was worried because her teacher said if she was late again, a note would be sent home to their parents. She told Drew, but he just laughed. Drew never seemed to get worried. When she got to her class, Cindy's teacher, Ms. Lopez, handed Cindy a note and told her to bring it home. Cindy was very upset. It was Drew's fault that they were late, but she was going to get in trouble. It was not fair! On the way home, she didn't even talk to her brother. When Drew and Cindy's parents came home from work, Cindy handed them the note. She waited while they read it, ready to explain herself. After reading the note, Cindy's father yelled, "Drew! Come here! We need to talk about why you keep making your sister late for school!"

1 Why are Drew and Cindy late for school so often?

○ **A** Cindy takes too long to get ready.

○ **B** Drew sleeps through his alarm.

○ **C** The bus driver forgets to pick them up.

○ **D** Ms. Lopez gives them the wrong directions.

2 How does Cindy feel when her teacher gives her a note to bring home?

○ **F** Relieved

○ **G** Tired

○ **H** Angry

○ **I** Happy

MAP CHECK 1

Directions: Read the passage below, and then answer the questions that follow.

Sally Ride, the First American Woman in Space

1   Sally Ride was the first American woman to fly in space. Born in 1951 in Encino, California, Ride graduated from Stanford University. During college, Ride decided that she wanted to be an astronaut.

2   Ride began astronaut training in 1978. Out of thirty-four astronauts in training, only six were women. Ride says all of the astronauts treated one another with respect: "The men in the group were very supportive and considered us as equals."

3   Astronaut training was very challenging. Ride had to become an expert on every detail of the space shuttle and the experiments. "It's a lot like being in school in a very difficult course," she said, "where you have to master everything."

4   Before going into space, Ride worked as support crew for other shuttle voyages. She got her first opportunity to go into space in 1983 aboard the space shuttle Challenger. The space shuttle took off from the Kennedy Space Center in Florida. It stayed in orbit for 147 hours and landed in California.

5   Ride served as flight engineer on her first shuttle ride. Along with two other astronauts, she helped to launch and land the shuttle. She was also responsible for operating the shuttle's robot arm. "The way you worked the robot arm," Ride explained, "is by using two hand controllers: One moves the arm up and down and to the side, and the other rotates it."

6   Ride said the takeoff was more exciting than the landing. "Liftoff is very exciting!" she said. "There really isn't time to be scared, but it's exhilarating and sometimes overwhelming."

7   She was very lucky because she didn't get sick in space. About half of the astronauts do get sick, Ride said. "The good news is that they all report that it goes away in a day or two and then they feel fine for the rest of the mission."

8   Ride is currently a physics professor at the University of California, San Diego. She encourages all her students to consider studying science. "Whether it's as an astronaut or an engineer in mission control or a scientist receiving data from Mars, there are lots of exciting possibilities," she said. "The most important thing is to get a good background in science while you're in school."

Whenever you see a multiple-choice question, you should first try to get rid of as many answer choices as you can. Then go back and choose from the ones that are left.

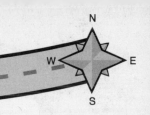

1 This article is mostly about what Sally Ride —

○ A wanted to become as a child

○ B did as an astronaut

○ C tells students to study

○ D teaches as a professor

2 Which one of the details below indicate that this is a nonfiction article?

○ F Space travel makes some people sick.

○ G Sally Ride wanted to be an astronaut.

○ H Few women have traveled to space.

○ J Sally Ride is an actual person.

3 The idea that fewer women than men are astronauts is *best* supported by which *fact* from the selection?

○ A Ride encourages both boys and girls to study science while they are in school.

○ B Ride didn't decide that she wanted to become an astronaut until she was in college.

○ C Ride said that the men in the training program were nice to the women.

○ D Only six of the thirty-four people training to become astronauts were women when Ride was training.

4 Which of the following sentences would *best* end paragraph 8?

○ F Most astronauts adjust to being in space and stop getting sick.

○ G More information about Sally Ride's life is available on the Internet.

○ H Ride believes all students should shoot for the stars.

○ J NASA is currently working with other countries to build a space station.

5 You know that training to be an astronaut is very difficult because of the *fact* that astronauts —

○ A must learn about all the details of the space shuttle

○ B become physically sick while they are in space

○ C graduate at the top of their class from Stanford University

○ D work on the support crews of other voyages

6 "First Shuttle Ride" is the *best* heading for which paragraph?

○ F 2

○ G 3

○ H 4

○ J 5

Directions: Read the passage below, and then answer the questions that follow.

The Combination

1 While my father was away on a fishing trip, he left a combination lock and a note on the dining room table. We found them when we arrived on the island.

2 According to the note, my father had programmed the lock but forgotten the combination. He thought he'd set the combination to a number that would be easy to remember, but he had somehow forgotten it.

3 The combination could be his birthday, or the year he was born. Or it could be my mother's birthday, or it could be the year of one of our birthdays. He was offering a $20 reward to the person who could crack the combination. Always eager to make some money, my brother Bart grabbed the lock first.

4 He fiddled with the lock for over an hour. "What was the year Father was born?" Bart asked my mother and me as we cooked dinner.

5 "1942," my mother answered.

6 But that didn't work. Soon, after Bart tried every possible combination of our birthdays, he threw the lock down in disgust.

7 The next day, I put the lock in my pocket and carried it down to the marina to try to earn the $20 reward as I watched the boats come sailing in. I flicked some numbers into place, and then yanked the lock, hoping it would open. But it didn't budge. Once the wind came up and foam started frosting the sea, I gave up and walked home.

8 That evening, my mother sat out on the deck, taking her turn at trying to crack the mystery. Her brow was knit in concentration as she spun the lock's numbers. She worked until the sun slipped behind a nearby island.

9 "Let's put our heads together," my mother announced to us, "and see whether we can think the way Father thinks."

10 The three of us gathered back on the deck, trying to think like our forgetful father. Overhead, seagulls squawked.

11 Mother spoke first. "He has a terrible habit of reversing numbers. Instead of writing 19, he sometimes writes 91."

12 "And sometimes he gets confused and thinks I was born in 1974, instead of 1984," my brother said.

13 "I have an idea," I said. "What if he mixed up the year of Bart's birthday, reversed it, and programmed in 4791?"

14 Mother spun the numbers into place, while my brother and I waited to see what would happen. Sure enough, the lock opened! And since the three of us had solved the puzzle together, we split the money into thirds.

When you're answering main idea questions, make sure you don't get tricked by answer choices that provide a detail from the passage. The best answer choice should provide a summary of the passage.

Tip

7 "The Reward" might be the *best* heading for which paragraph?

○ **A** 2

○ **B** 3

○ **C** 4

○ **D** 6

8 Which of the following sentences would be the *best* ending for paragraph 7?

○ **F** We had a wonderful time, and my father's problem was solved.

○ **G** Bart was always eager to make some money.

○ **H** My father was very absent-minded.

○ **J** I had no idea what the combination was.

9 Another good title for this story might be —

○ **A** "An Island Vacation"

○ **B** "Bart Goes First and Fails"

○ **C** "The Power of Working Together"

○ **D** "Mother's Attempt at the Combination"

10 Which sentences below *best* supports to the conclusion that the family lives near the sea?

○ **F** That evening, my mother sat out on the deck, taking her turn at trying to crack the mystery.

○ **G** Once the wind came up and foam started frosting the sea, I gave up and walked home.

○ **H** The three of us gathered back on the deck, trying to think like our forgetful father.

○ **J** While my father was away on a fishing trip, he left a combination lock and a note on the dining room table.

11 Which heading *best* describes the main idea of paragraph 8?

○ **A** The Challenge

○ **B** Giving Up

○ **C** Solving the Puzzle

○ **D** Mother's Attempt

12 You can infer that Bart is eager to claim the reward for himself from the *fact* that he —

○ **F** is the first to try to figure out the combination

○ **G** splits the reward money with his sibling and mother

○ **H** doesn't know the date of his father's birth

○ **J** knows his father sometimes confuses numbers

Directions: Read the passage below, and then answer the questions that follow.

Dreaming of Cake

1   Laura peeked out from curtains that separated her bedroom from the rest of the one-room sod cabin. Her parents were sitting on two barrels, their only furniture besides several trunks that served as tables. They didn't have much, but the cabin was comforting after their long journey to the wilds of Kansas. They'd begun decorating the walls with advertisements from the newspaper. Laura was also making a rag carpet to cover the dirt floor. Her parents both looked very serious. Laura listened quietly to what they were saying.

2   "We haven't had a drop of rain in many, many months," her father said in a low, serious voice. "I had hoped we might have a storm last night when I saw the lightning in the distance, but it was only the heat."

3   Laura's mother leaned forward and a look of fear flashed across her face. "What are we going to do? I used the last of the wheat in last night's supper. The potatoes ran out last week. We have several bags of cornmeal, but it is not enough to get us through the winter. I don't know what I am going to feed the children."

4   Laura knew that things were difficult. For the last couple days, she had gone out to gather wild acorns and other nuts. All the food that remained in the pantry were a couple of jars of preserved plums and stewed tomatoes. Laura hated stewed tomatoes, but she didn't complain when her mother served them for supper.

5   "Don't get alarmed," Laura heard her father say. "I've heard that some people are collecting food and money to help Kansas farmers survive the drought. I think I should go to Kansas City and get some corn and flour. It's our only hope to survive the winter."

6   Laura couldn't muffle her cry. The journey to Kansas City was long, and her father could be gone a long time. Laura remembered the huge snowdrifts from last year. Some of them were so big they had to dig tunnels through them to get from the cabin to the barn. She wanted her father to stay, but she knew they had no choice.

7   Laura crept quietly back to her bed. She shut her eyes and willed herself to think of something happy. When her father returned from Kansas City, they would make a buttermilk cake to celebrate his return. As she fell asleep, her mouth started to water. She would think about her mother's wonderful cake while her father was gone.

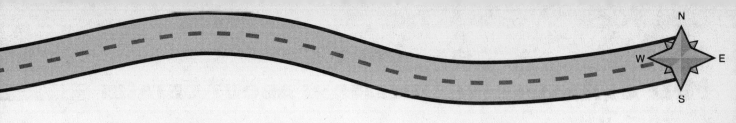

13 What detail below can you use to tell that the story is probably historical fiction?

- ○ **A** There has been a shortage of rain.
- ○ **B** Laura shares a room with her parents.
- ○ **C** The family lives in a sod cabin.
- ○ **D** It snows a lot in the winter.

14 The main idea of this story is that—

- ○ **F** Laura is listening to her parents' conversation
- ○ **G** the family lives in a small sod cabin
- ○ **H** farmers can get free food in Kansas City
- ○ **J** Laura's family is running out of food

15 The idea that Laura helps out the family with important chores is *best* supported by which information from the passage?

- ○ **A** Their father has to go to Kansas City for food.
- ○ **B** Laura collects acorns and other nuts.
- ○ **C** Laura listens to her parents' conversation.
- ○ **D** Laura eats stewed tomatoes even though she doesn't like them.

16 "Long Drought" might be the *best* heading for which paragraph?

- ○ **F** 1
- ○ **G** 2
- ○ **H** 3
- ○ **J** 4

17 Which sentence below *best* completes paragraph 6?

- ○ **A** The table would be bare if her father didn't make the journey.
- ○ **B** Laura wanted to listen to every word they said.
- ○ **C** She wanted her parents to come with her to gather nuts.
- ○ **D** She fell into a deep sleep dreaming about the cake they would eat.

18 Which of the following headings *best* describes paragraph 5?

- ○ **F** Eavesdropping
- ○ **G** Winter Challenges
- ○ **H** Kansas City
- ○ **J** Free Food

Tip

Even if you think that the first answer choice is correct, be sure to read *every* answer choice before choosing a final response. You may find a better answer if you continue reading the other choices.

MILE 6: ANSWERING QUESTIONS ABOUT DETAILS

Some questions will ask you about details from a passage. These questions can be easy to answer if you remember to do three things after you read the passage.

- Read the question and find out what you need to know to answer the question.

- Skim the passage looking for key words from the question.

- Reread the section of the passage where the answer is located.

Don't try to memorize all of the information from the passage. You don't need to, because you can always go back and read to find the answer.

Directions: Read each of the short passages below and answer the questions that follow. Underline the phrase or sentence in each passage that supports your response.

Eunice had a terrible thing happen to her when she reached camp. She couldn't open her suitcase! She had forgotten to ask her parents for the code to the suitcase lock before she left. Her suitcase contained everything she needed for the summer. She didn't know what to do!

Eunice tried calling home, but no one answered. She jumped on the suitcase, thinking it might pop open. But that didn't work. Just when she was about to cry, she remembered that her mother had given her a card. She hoped the card would cheer her up. When she opened the card she saw that her mother had written, in large letters, "Don't forget the combination. It's 461."

1. **Why did Eunice open the card from her mother?**

_____

_____

Rubber is one of the most important materials in the world. It's waterproof; it doesn't conduct electricity; it holds air and repels water; and it can block out or muffle noise. Without rubber, you couldn't ride a bike, wear sneakers, or water the lawn with a garden hose.

Europeans only discovered rubber when they began exploring Central and South America more than four hundred years ago. They found native Central and South Americans playing a game with a bouncing ball. Upon further investigation, they learned that the ball was made from a white liquid produced by a rubber tree.

2. Why is rubber so important?

_____

_____

As Dmitri strummed his guitar, he thought about his grandfather. His grandfather, Irving, had taught him to play the instrument. Irving had given Dmitri his first guitar when Dmitri was in second grade. Dmitri recalled sitting on his grandfather's front porch learning different chords. He studied his grandfather's long fingers while he played, and he listened to the notes.

"If you learn to play the guitar," his grandfather said, "you can spread joy wherever you go."

Dmitri often grew frustrated with his clumsy fingers. They couldn't seem to reach the right combinations of strings.

"Patience," his grandfather said. "Learning to spread joy with music takes time and practice. But you'll learn it's well worth the effort."

3. Why did Dmitri get frustrated when he was learning to play the guitar?

_____

_____

The word "quicksand" is enough to strike fear into the hearts of many people. In countless scary movies, characters have stepped into quicksand and then vanished, pulled into the ground by the mysterious substance.

Actually, there's nothing very mysterious about quicksand. Quicksand can be made of sand or soil that has water flowing up through it. That means you'll never find quicksand on a beach because the water is flowing down through the sand. Instead, valleys, bogs, riverbeds, and streambeds are the most likely places you'll encounter quicksand. That's because the sand or soil is floating on the water that is beneath it.

4. Where are the *most* likely places to find quicksand?

_____

_____

Skimming is an important skill. It means reading quickly to find key words or to get a sense of an article or story.

Directions: Read the questions on the following page, and then skim the selection to help you answer the questions.

Preventing Stitches

1   Have you ever had to stop running because your side started to hurt? Do you ever get a stitch in your side?

2   Side stitches are muscle spasms. They occur in the diaphragm. The diaphragm is a muscle below your lungs that helps you breathe. When you inhale, drawing air into your lungs, the diaphragm moves down. When you exhale, breathing out, the diaphragm moves up. Sometimes, your internal organs pull and push against the diaphragm. This causes a muscle spasm or a side stitch.

3   The liver, the largest organ in the abdomen, usually causes side stitches. It is attached to the diaphragm by two ligaments. Because it's on the right side, most people get stitches on their right side. Stitches also occur if you run right after eating.

4   Another cause of stitches is the way you run and breathe. Most people inhale and exhale on the same foot. This means that you might exhale every fourth time your foot hits the ground. Every time you exhale, the diaphragm moves up. At the same time, your foot hitting the ground causes your internal organs to move down. Therefore, they pull against the diaphragm, causing a muscle spasm or stitch.

5   "There are many different ways to prevent side stitches," says Lourdes Santos, a veteran runner. "Side stitches don't have to ruin your runs."

6   The best strategy is to stop "shallow" breathing. Shallow breathing means you are taking in a small amount of air and not filling your lungs completely. When this happens, your diaphragm never moves down completely. Thus, the liver is always pulling against it.

7   There is a way, called "belly breathing," that can ensure you're breathing deeply.

8   **Belly Breathing:** Lie on the floor. Put your hand on your stomach. Take a deep breath of air. If your hand moves up slightly, then you are breathing deeply. If your hand doesn't move and only your chest moves, you are not filling your lungs with enough air.

9   There are other tricks you can try while running to prevent stitches. One is to purse your lips and pretend you are blowing out birthday candles. You can only do this if you are breathing deeply. Another is to exhale when your left foot hits the ground. The organs on the left side of the body are smaller. They won't put as much strain on the diaphragm.

5. What is one of the causes of side stitches? _____

_____

_____

6. How can you tell if you're breathing deeply? _____

_____

_____

7. Why do some people pretend they're blowing out candles while they run?

_____

_____

_____

8. Why does shallow breathing cause side stitches? _____

_____

_____

_____

9. What are the steps to "belly breathing"? _____

_____

_____

MILE 7: LEARNING VOCABULARY IN CONTEXT

Landmarks help you find your way when you're on a journey. You might know you are going in the right direction when you cross a certain river or see a certain building. The same is true when you're reading. You may see a word that you don't understand. However, the sentence in which the word appears and the sentences before and after it usually provide clues about the definition of the word. This is considered learning vocabulary in context.

Directions: Read the following passage. Use clues to figure out the meaning of the underlined words. After reading, look at page 37. Match the vocabulary words in column 1 with their definitions in column 2.

Twins

1   Ben and Naomi are brother and sister. They were born only four minutes apart. That makes them twins. However, they don't look anything alike. They also don't share any of the same interests.

2   Twins often look so much alike that you can't tell them apart. They may also share the same interests such as reading. Sometimes they'll have the same <u>mannerisms</u>. For example, if one twin moves his or her hands a certain way when he or she talks, the other twin probably does too.

3   There are two kinds of twins: fraternal and identical twins. Ben and Naomi are fraternal twins. This means that two separate sperm fertilized two separate eggs. This is rare because women's bodies usually only release one egg at a time. In fact, about one in ninety Caucasian women will have fraternal twins. Among other groups, the rate is higher. One in seventy-eight African American or Native American women have fraternal twins.

4   Even more rare are <u>identical</u> twins. Identical twins share the same physical characteristics such as gender, hair color, birth weight, and height. This occurs when a fertilized egg splits in two. As a result, identical twins have the same genetic material—the chemical molecules that determine your physical traits. The causes of eggs splitting and creating identical twins are still a mystery. It happens about one time for every 250 births.

5   For years, people have debated why people act certain ways. Some argue that people are shaped primarily by <u>heredity</u>, the qualities genetically inherited from their parents. Others believe that people are more influenced by <u>environmental</u> factors such as their surroundings, friends, community, and income.

6   Researchers used twins to explore this debate by finding identical twins who had been separated and raised by different sets of parents. Because the twins shared the same <u>genetic material</u>—the chemical structure inside the blood—but had been raised in different homes, researchers hoped to explore how similar or different they were.

7   The results were surprising. Comparing <u>traits</u>, such as intelligence, behavior, and values, researchers found that the twins were very similar, even though they had grown up in separate places. This means that heredity influences human behavior in some very important categories.

COLUMN 1

mannerisms

identical

genetic material

heredity

environmental

traits

COLUMN 2

inherited qualities

circumstantial

characteristics

exactly alike

habits

chemical molecules

MILE 8: PREFIXES AND SUFFIXES = - - - - - - - - - - -

A **prefix** is a word part that you add to the beginning of a word. It changes the meaning of the word. For example, you can change the word "like" to become "dislike" by adding the prefix "dis" to the beginning of the word. The new word means the opposite of the base word.

Directions: The selection below is missing some words. Fill in the nine blank spots with a word you create by matching a prefix with a base word from the box below. Each base word is used once. The first example has been done for you.

Prefixes:	dis-	re-	un-	pre-	
Base Words:	-appeared	-start	-school	-liked	-read
	happy	-heat	-adjust	-turn	

I remember my first day of ____preschool____. It was terrible! My mother took me into the classroom where I started playing with blocks. But when I discovered that she had _____, I started crying. I was very _____! The teacher offered to read me a book, but my mother had already read me the book, and I did not want to _____ it.

Once I realized that my situation wouldn't change, I wiped away my tears. Though I was very young, I knew I had to _____ my attitude and try to make some friends.

I saw a little boy playing in the sandbox and decided to join him. But as soon I picked up a shovel, he threw sand in my eyes! This caused my tears to _____ flowing. I _____ everyone, and everyone seemed to hate me. I just wanted to _____ home to where I had my own toys.

Luckily, a little girl walked up to me at that moment and said, "Don't cry. Come and play house with me."

A huge smile spread across my face. "Can we bake cookies?" I asked.

"Of course," she said, scampering off toward the play kitchen. "I'll _____ the oven while you make the cookie dough."

The little girl's name was Lydia, and she became my best friend for the school year.

A **suffix** is a word part that you add to the end of a word. It changes the meaning of the word. For example, you can change the word "own" to "owner" by adding the suffix "er" to the end of the word.

Directions: The selection below is missing some words. Fill in the eight blank spots with a word you create by matching a suffix with a base word from the box below. Each base word is used once. The first example has been done for you.

Base Words:	bad-	hope-	loud-	care-
	firm-	filth-	believe-	sudden-
Suffixes:	-less	-able	-ly	-ful	-y

Lisette wanted to go to a movie very ___badly___, but her mother wouldn't let her. "Not until you clean your room," her mother said _____.

Lisette looked at her room. There were dirty clothes on her bed and dirty dishes under it. Last week, she had been _____ and spilled a container of glitter on the floor. There were even some cobwebs in the corner. She thought it was _____ to try and clean this _____ room.

"I wish I had a cleaning fairy," Lisette thought to herself. "Someone who would _____ appear and make this mess vanish."

Lisette pushed her clothes off her bed, lay down, and fell asleep. Then she heard someone whispering in her ear. "Lisette, this is your cleaning fairy," someone said.

Lisette rubbed her eyes. It was simply not _____! An old woman dressed in rags was standing in her room.

"What you are doing in my room?" Lisette screamed _____.

"I'm here to clean your room," the old woman cackled. She bent down to pick a sock off the floor, and her back cracked noisily. "Ouch!" the woman cried. "There goes my back."

Lisette looked at the woman and felt horrible. She couldn't let the strange woman clean her mess. She sprang off her bed, shouting, "I'll do it myself. Sit down and rest. It won't take me long at all."

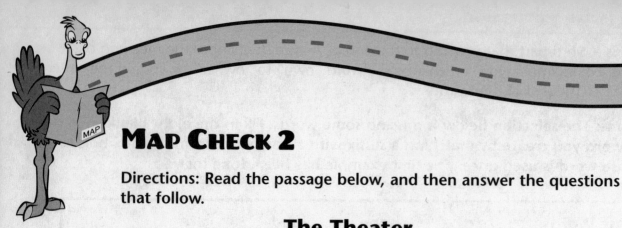

MAP CHECK 2

Directions: Read the passage below, and then answer the questions that follow.

The Theater

1 Today we took a field trip to a theater where plays are put on. There is so much more to the theater than I ever imagined.

2 Theater buildings are divided into three different areas: the stage, the auditorium, and the backstage area.

3 The stage is where the actors perform the play. We learned that there are three different types of stages. The oldest <u>type</u> is an arena stage. When actors perform on an arena stage, the audience surrounds them. Arena stages were used more than 2,000 years ago. When the audience surrounds three sides of the stage it is a thrust stage. Scenery is placed against the fourth side. The final kind of stage is a proscenium or "picture frame" stage. The audience sits in front of the stage, which is located underneath an arch.

4 The auditorium is where the audience sits. Some auditoriums have orchestra pits, a submerged area directly in front of the stage where the musicians play their instruments. Other auditoriums have a second level, which is called the mezzanine or balcony.

5 As you can guess, the backstage area is behind the stage. This is where the actors prepare for the play. Props are stored in the prop room. We spent thirty minutes exploring in the prop room. It was filled with all kinds of interesting stuff. One of my friends found several fake swords, and I discovered an old-fashioned gum ball machine.

6 After we finished our tour, we visited different people who work in the theater. First, we talked to a playwright. Playwrights are very important. They write the plays. Another important person is the producer. Producers choose the plays to be performed, raise the money to pay for the plays, hire the directors, and pay all the bills.

7 The director is responsible for the quality of the play. He or she reads and interprets the play, selects the actors for the parts, and oversees the transformation of the written play into dramatic action. The director also <u>oversees</u> all aspects of the production, including the scenery, lighting, music, and costumes.

8 Of course, the actors are the most visible people who work in the theater. Many people think that acting is easy. However, the actors told us that acting is hard work. Many of them have acted for years, taking courses on voice (to pronounce words loudly and clearly), characterization (to understand different kinds of people), and body movement (to move on stage).

Tip

When you're answering main idea questions, make sure you don't get tricked by answer choices that provide a detail from the passage. The best answer choice should provide a summary of the passage.

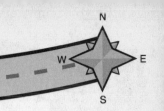

1 The narrator enjoyed the field trip to the theater because he or she —

○ **A** got to meet many famous actors and actresses

○ **B** believes that plays are much more enjoyable than movies

○ **C** saw that the theater involves many different parts and people

○ **D** always wanted to become a well-known playwright

2 The passage contains the following phrase:

> **the director also oversees all aspects of production**

Which one of the following words uses <u>or</u> in the same meaning as the <u>or</u> in dire<u>or</u>?

○ **F** tail<u>or</u>

○ **G** n<u>or</u>th

○ **H** do<u>or</u>

○ **J** <u>or</u>ange

3 In the third paragraph, the word <u>type</u> means —

○ **A** family

○ **B** classify

○ **C** copy

○ **D** kind

4 The students spent a lot of time in the prop room because they —

○ **F** found interesting objects in the room

○ **G** dressed up like pirates and had a sword fight

○ **H** wanted to get some gum from the machine

○ **J** were tired of touring the theater

5 The word <u>oversees</u> in paragraph 7 is used so that it means —

○ **A** looks at

○ **B** stands over

○ **C** manages

○ **D** views

6 Producers are responsible for —

○ **F** helping the actors to strengthen their voices

○ **G** managing the business side of plays

○ **H** interpreting the play and selecting actors

○ **J** suggesting topics to playwrights

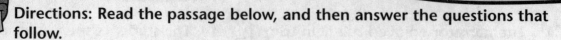

Directions: Read the passage below, and then answer the questions that follow.

Spelunking

1   When Daniel and Lydia ducked into the entrance of the cavern, they didn't know what to expect. They were on a spelunking expedition with Lydia's father. Spelunkers are people who explore caverns and caves. It's an exciting hobby that takes people to unexplored or out-of-the-way places.

2   "It's time to turn on your miner's headlamp," Lydia's father said. "Today, we're going to be exploring a cavern."

3   "What's the difference between a cavern and a cave?" Daniel asked.

4   "Great question," Lydia's father said as they put on their gloves and kneepads to protect themselves from any scrapes. "A cave can be any hollowed out area on the side of a hill or in the ground, but a cavern is a very large cave. Usually a cavern has at least one huge room. That's what we'll be looking for today."

5   The three began walking down a dark tunnel. Their headlamps provided just enough light to see the way. Caverns are generally found where there are large deposits of limestone. Limestone is a soft rock made from ancient remains of coral, mollusks, plankton, and other marine organisms. When water with small traces of carbonic acids falls on limestone, it begins to dissolve the rock by trickling into each <u>crack</u> and crevice. Over long periods of time, they become larger, eventually becoming cavities and caverns.

6   The three spelunkers knew that the cavern had once been filled with water. However, as the climate grew drier, the water disappeared—almost!

7   "Hey, I think I just stepped in a puddle!" Lydia squealed. Shining her flashlight down on the floor, she discovered a small stream running along the bottom of the passageway. It's not uncommon to find streams or even lakes underground.

8   Suddenly, Lydia's father stopped. "I can't believe it," he said excitedly.

9   Up ahead was a huge cavern with fifteen-foot-high ceilings. Hanging from the ceiling were beautiful formations that looked like icicles. Of course, they weren't really icicles. They were actually stalactites. Stalactites form when water drips from the ceiling of the cave. Each drop of water leaves behind a hard substance called calcite. Eventually, the calcite builds into an icicle.

10 Lydia shined her flashlight on the ground. "Look," she cried, "there are stalactites on the floor also."

11 Lydia's father laughed. "Not quite. The structures growing from the floor are called stalagmites. Sometimes, stalagmites and stalactites join and form columns."

12 Daniel's flashlight traveled around the room. "Is that one?" Illuminated by the light were three rock columns.

13 "Yep!" Lydia's father's voice echoed in the cavern. "This place is amazing!"

You don't need to memorize all the information in a passage. When you're answering a question, just skim the part of the passage you think will provide the answer. Then read that part carefully.

Tip

7 In paragraph 5, the word <u>crack</u> is used to mean —

○ **A** snap

○ **B** comment

○ **C** gap

○ **D** sound

8 Look at this phrase from the article:

> eventual<u>ly</u> becoming cavities and caverns

The <u>ly</u> in eventual<u>ly</u> shares the same meaning as the <u>ly</u> in which word below?

○ **F** doi<u>ly</u>

○ **G** loud<u>ly</u>

○ **H** hol<u>ly</u>

○ **J** <u>ly</u>rical

9 Daniel, Lydia, and Lydia's father turn on their miner's headlamps because —

○ **A** they are looking for gold and silver

○ **B** they must protect their heads

○ **C** they enjoy turning them on

○ **D** caves are underground and dark

10 If you skimmed this article, you would —

○ **F** ask your best friend to read it to you

○ **G** memorize the beginning and end

○ **H** only read the dialogue and nothing else

○ **J** read quickly for the main ideas

11 The meaning of <u>expedition</u> in paragraph 1 is —

○ **A** business

○ **B** journey

○ **C** exam

○ **D** recess

12 Why is Lydia's father so excited at the end of the article?

○ **F** They discover that some stalagmites and stalactites have joined to become columns.

○ **G** Lydia spots the largest underwater lake he's ever seen.

○ **H** He is surprised to find out that Lydia and Daniel like spelunking as much as he does.

○ **J** They have found a hidden mine that is full of gold and will make them rich.

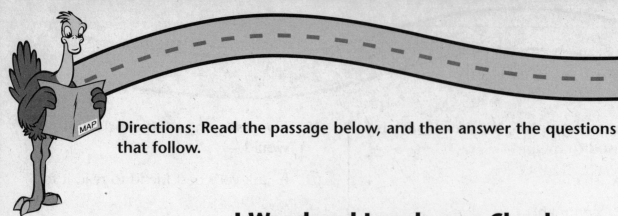

Directions: Read the passage below, and then answer the questions that follow.

I Wandered Lonely as a Cloud

by William Wordsworth

1   I wandered lonely as a cloud
2   That floats on high o'er vales and hills,
3   When all at once I saw a crowd,
4   A <u>host</u>, of golden daffodils;
5   Beside the lake, beneath the trees,
6   Fluttering and dancing in the breeze.

7   Continuous as the stars that shine
8   And twinkle on the milky way,
9   They stretched in never-ending line
10   Along the margin of a bay:
11   Ten thousand saw I at a glance,
12   Tossing their heads in sprightly dance.

13   The waves beside them danced; but they
14   Out-did the sparkling waves in glee;
15   A poet could not but be gay,
16   In such a jocund company;
17   I gazed—and gazed—but little thought
18   What wealth the show to me had brought:

19   For oft, when on my couch I lie
20   In vacant or in <u>pensive</u> mood,
21   They flash upon that inward eye
22   Which is the bliss of solitude;
23   And then my heart with pleasure fills,
24   And dances with the daffodils.

When you're reading poetry, read slowly and carefully. Make sure you understand each line before continuing to the next one.

Tip

13 If you wanted to find out what the poet thinks about as he lies on his couch, you could —

○ **A** skim for the part where the poet goes to sleep

○ **B** skim the poem until you find the word couch

○ **C** memorize the second stanza of the poem

○ **D** read the poem aloud to a friend and discuss it

14 Look at this line from the poem:

> They flash upon that <u>in</u>ward eye

In which word is <u>in</u> used in the same way as <u>in</u>ward above?

○ **F** listen<u>in</u>g

○ **G** <u>in</u>coming

○ **H** <u>in</u>definite

○ **J** f<u>in</u>d

15 The poet's heart fills with pleasure when he —

○ **A** floats like a cloud

○ **B** thinks of the daffodils

○ **C** picks flowers for his wife

○ **D** swims in the ocean

16 Another word for <u>host</u> in line 4 of the poem would be —

○ **F** plant

○ **G** entertainer

○ **H** mass

○ **J** wafer

17 Look at this line from the poem.

> Tossing their heads in spright<u>ly</u> dance

In which word below is <u>ly</u> used the same way as it is in spright<u>ly</u>?

○ **A** high<u>ly</u>

○ **B** fami<u>ly</u>

○ **C** <u>ly</u>rical

○ **D** <u>ly</u>nx

18 In line 20, the word <u>pensive</u> could be replaced with —

○ **F** talkative

○ **G** heavy

○ **H** thoughtful

○ **J** vacationing

MILE 9: MAKING PREDICTIONS

Making a prediction means using clues to figure out what is going to happen. If you see dark clouds in the sky and hear thunder, your prediction could be that it will rain. You can also make predictions when you read. Clues in a selection can help you figure out what might happen next.

Directions: Read the first part of a passage below and answer the questions on the next page. Then read the rest of the story and see how close your predictions were.

The Boy Who Always Went First

THE STORY...

1   On the 75th floor of a very tall apartment building lived a boy named Ugali Zonta. Everywhere Ugali went, and everything he did, he always insisted that he should go first. When he entered the elevator to whisk him up to his apartment, he cut in front of the other people waiting. You would think that someone might have shouted, "Young man, what on earth are you doing?" but no one did because Ugali had the most charming smile. His teeth were straight and white, and he had a nickel-sized dimple on each cheek. His eyes, the color of milk chocolate, sparkled when he smiled. Ugali's smile made people feel like they were being bathed in sunlight.

2   So Ugali went through life stepping to the front of lines, helping himself to the biggest pieces of cake, always getting the best ball or jump rope at recess. He would get the best seats at movies, and he never waited outside in the rain. As you can imagine, this made some of his classmates envious.

3   "I don't understand it," said Abel Aptner. "Both of my names begin with 'A.' It's not fair that Ugali, whose last name begins with 'Z,' should always go first."

4   "I agree," Cassius Coleman said. "Ugali thinks his smile is as good as gold, but I don't care that he has perfect teeth and has never worn braces. That doesn't mean he has the right to cut in line."

5   "Everyone thinks he's cute because of his dimples," Abel said. "I've got dimples." Abel poked his cheek with his finger. "If I press hard enough, I've got very cute dimples."

6   When Ugali's class played kickball at recess, the teacher chose two kids as captains, and the two captains, in turn, chose their teams. Ugali was a very good kickball player. In fact, he always kicked the ball so far into left field that he made home runs every time. So he was always chosen first for kickball games when he wasn't one of the captains.

7   Here was a situation that Cassius and Abel decided they could control. "The next time we're captains of the kickball teams," Abel said to Cassius, "neither of us will choose Ugali. Deal?" Abel stuck out his hand for Cassius to shake.

8   "Deal," Cassius answered, shaking Abel's hand.

1. **What do you think is going to happen next in this story?**

_____

_____

_____

2. **How do you think the story is going to turn out?**

_____

_____

_____

3. **Write down one question that the conclusion of the story should answer.**

_____

_____

_____

4. **Write down a second question that the conclusion of the story should answer.**

_____

_____

_____

THE CONCLUSION...

1 Of course, Cassius and Abel had to wait several weeks before their teacher, Ms. Wong, asked them both to be captains on the same day. When she called their names from her list and made them captains, they quickly glanced at each other, smiled, and nodded. Once in the hallway, the two boys gave each other high fives and ran outside for recess.

2 As usual, the whole class was gathered. And, as usual, Ugali was smiling his famous smile. Everyone was smiling back at him. Cassius and Abel flipped a coin to see who would choose first, and Abel won. He coughed, then cleared his throat. Before he uttered a word, Ugali began to walk toward him.

3 "Save your voice," Ugali said boastfully.

4 "I pick Dixon," Abel shouted.

5 Ugali froze in place. Dixon was the second-best kickball player in the class.

6 "Well," Ugali said in a peevish way before he began walking toward Cassius.

7 Cassius bit his lip and pushed his hair off his forehead. "I choose Jackie."

8 Someone shouted, "Wacky Jackie?"

9 Jackie was the worst kickball player. Sometimes, he closed his eyes as the ball rolled closer, and he would miss it completely.

10 Ugali stood, opening and closing his fists, and his face turned beet red. Cassius and Abel could tell he was furious. They exchanged glances. What if a fight started? How humiliating would it be if Ugali beat up both of them? "Liz," Abel whispered. "Liz is on my team."

11 "Jeremiah," Cassius called out next.

12 As the two continued to call out names, the most astonishing thing happened. Ugali began to cry. With his face crumpled like a paper bag, he looked human again. Yes, he had dimples, his smile was friendly, and his eyes sparkled, but when he was crying he looked like an ordinary boy. Both Cassius and Abel felt so bad that they almost lost their resolve, and they almost said they had meant to choose Ugali first.

13 They didn't, however, and instead the strangest thing happened. Ugali stomped his foot and declared, "I'm sick of kickball. It's a stupid game. Who wants to play tetherball with me?" Smiling weakly, he looked at the other kids and then turned and marched toward the tetherball courts. Everyone was too shocked to move.

14 From that day on, Ugali played tetherball by himself every day. You could say that he was the first to discover the game of tetherball on the playground, and he's still waiting for the other kids to come and play with him. When they finally do, he will be the first in line, and the first to explain the rules to them.

5. Summarize what happens at the end of the story.

_____

_____

_____

_____

6. How does the actual ending compare to what you thought was going to happen?

_____

_____

7. Write down the answer to the first question you wrote on page 49.

_____

_____

8. Write down the answer to the second question you wrote on page 49.

_____

_____

MILE 10: DRAWING CONCLUSIONS

Great job! Now that you've practiced making predictions, you're ready to draw your own conclusions. Drawing a conclusion is similar to making a prediction. In Mile 9, you used information to figure out what would happen next in a selection. Now you will figure out something about a character or selection based on what you read. Look at the example below.

"Sally smelled the bottle of perfume and frowned."

Making a Prediction: Sally will not buy the perfume.

Drawing a Conclusion: Sally does not like the smell of the perfume.

Directions: Look at the picture below. Then write four conclusions based on what's happening in the picture. Look at the individual players as well as the teams.

1. _____

2. _____

3. _____

4. _____

Directions: Ten people are waiting in line to buy tickets to the county fair. Their expressions, clothes, and possessions give clues about what they are doing at the fair. After studying each person, write one thing you can conclude about each person or pair in line.

1. _____
   _____
   _____

2. _____
   _____

3. _____
   _____

4. _____
   _____

5. _____

6. _____

7. _____

8. _____

Directions: Read the story below, paying close attention to the underlined sentences. Then answer the questions on the following page.

1   Tali didn't mean to upset the pig. After shoveling out the pen, she was hosing it down when she accidentally sprayed the pig with water. The pig squealed, then charged toward Tali, knocking her off her feet. <u>Tali screamed. She breathed in quick, short puffs of air.</u> The pig had knocked the wind out of her. She looked up. The pig was staring at her through its squinty pig eyes. It was strange. She'd always towered over the pig, and now it towered over her. <u>The pig's body was covered in sharp, bristly hair, and its nose was gross and slobbery. Its hooves looked razor sharp.</u> Tali felt her heart begin to hammer in her chest. The pig had a strange look in its eye.

2   "Help," Tali screamed. "Someone help me!"

3   The pig sniffed. Tali's father had told her it was important to remain calm around animals because they could smell your feelings. She tried to take a deep breath. Was it possible that the pig could smell her fear?

4   The pig sat down with a heavy sigh right near Tali's head, and Tali almost choked. The smell of muck and slop was overpowering. What was she going to do? If the pig rolled over, Tali's face would be pressed into its body. The thought made her stomach turn. She needed help, but how could she call for help without arousing the pig's suspicion?

5   Just then, she had an idea. She would trick the pig by singing a song for help. She licked her chapped lips, swallowed, and then began to sing.

6   "I'm trapped in the pigpen

With a very angry swine.

If you come and help me

I'm sure I will be fine.

<u>The pig got angry</u>

<u>And pushed me to the floor.</u>

<u>Won't you please come and help me</u>

<u>Escape through the door?"</u>

7   Tali sang the song sweetly and calmly, though her heart was pounding. Even though she was singing at the top of her lungs, the pig closed its eyes and began gently snoring. A thread of spit dribbled from its mouth.

8   Tali sat up quietly. No one had come to save her, but now was her chance to escape. Holding her breath, she tiptoed from the pen and the sleeping pig. When she was safely outside, she breathed a huge sigh of relief.

9   Living on a farm was always an adventure, but Tali hoped she never got stuck with the pig again.

---

1. **Based on the sentences below, how does Tali feel?**

   "Tali screamed. She breathed in quick, short puffs of air."

   _____

   _____

2. **Based on the sentences below, how does Tali feel about the pig?**

   "The pig's body was covered in sharp, bristly hair, and its nose was gross and slobbery. Its hooves looked razor sharp."

   _____

   _____

3. **Based on the sentences below, how will Tali feel if the pig rolls on her? What will she probably do?**

   "If the pig rolled over, Tali's face would be pressed into its body. The thought made her stomach turn."

   _____

   _____

4. **Based on the sentence below, why is Tali singing this song?**

   "The pig got angry / And pushed me to the floor. / Won't you please come and help me / Escape through the door?"

   _____

   _____

5. **Based on the sentence below, why does Tali leave the pen this way?**

   "Holding her breath, she tiptoed from the pen and the sleeping pig."

   _____

   _____

MILE 11: DRAWING CONCLUSIONS ABOUT AUTHORS' CHOICES

Take a deep breath. You've made it to the eleventh mile! Guess what—it's very similar to the tenth mile. To draw conclusions about authors' choices, look for clues in the passage and ask yourself questions like, "Why did the author use this example?" and "Why did the author use this description?"

Directions: Read the story below and answer the questions that follow.

Barnaby and Basil

1   An old man named Barnaby and his young daughter, Basil, woke one morning and found the tongue of the ocean licking their front doorstep. By noon, the salt water had crept into the front hallway and stained their Oriental rug.

2   Barnaby consulted his prized possession, an atlas, and then called his daughter to him. "Basil," he said, "the ocean is unhappy. It is time for us to pack our belongings and move to the forest."

3   Although her father had warned her that someday they would have to move, salty tears streamed down Basil's face. The ocean had been her constant companion. In the mornings, she strolled along the water's edge, looking for fancy shells and ribbons of seaweed to fashion into jewelry. In the afternoons, she sat in the small fort she'd built from driftwood. And in the evening, the ocean lulled her to sleep with its gentle sound.

4   Now, Basil looked out the smudged window of her father's house. She could tell the ocean was angry. It was metallic gray with dots of white foam. It pounded the sand, picking up and carrying away the driftwood. Her fort had disappeared, and Basil knew their house would soon follow. She took a deep breath. The salt still made her nose twitch, but now it also sent a shiver down her back.

5   Basil began gathering her most important possessions—her favorite shells and rocks, a quilt, binoculars, clothes, and books—while her father packed up the rest of the house. Then the pair set off for the forest. The path was long and steep, but they never looked back, even when they climbed to the top of the hill, a place that had once been their favorite place from which to survey the ocean. Both of their hearts would have broken to see the ocean behaving so violently.

6   After walking for many days, they finally reached the forest. Barnaby built a house from small logs while Basil carved furniture. At first, they were each so busy working on their house they didn't have time to think about leaving the ocean. But on the fifth night, Basil didn't fall asleep after sliding into bed. She lay there listening. The silence made her miss the lullaby of the ocean, and she couldn't sleep. In fact, she was up all night, and she watched the sun rise above the trees and wished they hadn't left their ocean home.

7 It was like this every night for a month. Dark moons grew under Basil's eyes, and she stopped speaking, except to say "yes" or "no." Summer turned into fall, and one night as Basil lay in bed, her father came into her room.

8 "Listen carefully, Basil," he said. "The sound is there if you listen."

9 Basil cupped her hand around her ear and listened. At first, she heard nothing but her heart beating and air whistling in and out of her teeth. Then, she heard a whisper.

10 "It's the wind in the trees," her father explained. "It reminds me of the ocean in its gentle years."

11 And sure enough Basil could hear it—the wind flowing through the leaves and needle of the trees, like water flowing over sand. Her lips turned into a smile, and before she could say goodnight to her father, she had fallen fast asleep.

1. **Explain how the author makes the story enjoyable to read.**

_____

_____

_____

2. **Why does the author include examples in the third paragraph of all the different activities that Basil does near the ocean?**

_____

_____

_____

3. **The author writes, "dark moons grew under Basil's eyes." What does this line tell you about Basil?**

_____

_____

4. **What effect does the last line have on the story?**

_____

_____

_____

Authors write for many different purposes. They can write to provide information or to persuade the reader. They may want to entertain or to share an experience.

Directions: Read the opening sentences of the selections below. Then answer the questions about their purpose that follow.

> Sleepyhead, sleepyhead, lying asleep
>
> Sleepyhead, sleepyhead, snoring like sheep
>
> The day is a-wasting, and you'll be blue
>
> If you ruin it dozing all the day through

5. **What was the author's purpose in writing this selection?** _____

_____

6. **How does the repeating word "sleepyhead" contribute to the author's purpose?**

_____

_____

You can't argue with the facts. Wearing a seatbelt saves lives. In fact, seatbelts save the lives of about 9,500 people each year. In contrast, one American dies every hour because he or she didn't wear a seatbelt. It doesn't take much to do something that will save your life. The next time you get in a car, remember to buckle up.

7. **What was the author's purpose in writing this selection?** _____

_____

8. **How does the fact that "seatbelts save the lives of approximately 9,500 people each year" contribute to the author's purpose?**

_____

_____

Lee handed her mother a cluster of seaweed. "What's this?" her mother asked.

"Seaweed cocktail," Lee answered sweetly. "It's nice and fresh. I pulled it from the ocean this morning."

Her mother choked and her eyes opened wide. "You want me to eat it?"

Lee rolled her eyes and said, "Everyone knows that it's good for you. Haven't you ever heard of sushi?"

9. What was the author's purpose in writing this selection? _____

_____

10. How does the description of the mother's reaction to the seaweed contribute to the author's purpose? _____

_____

The Appalachian Mountains were more amazing than I imagined. My family had spent the last two days walking into the foothills of the mountain range. My Dad said we would hike about ten miles every day, taking mid-afternoon breaks for lunch. But he didn't mention that we would be walking up and down so much! The trails didn't just traverse the side of the mountain; they were usually incredibly steep. By the end of the second day, my feet were covered in blisters, and I could barely put on my boots.

11. What was the author's purpose in writing this selection? _____

_____

12. How does knowing about the author's blisters contribute to the author's purpose?

_____

_____

The Scottish physicist, Sir David Brewster, invented kaleidoscopes in 1816. A kaleidoscope is an optical instrument that presents changing patterns. It is a toy to some people, a new glimpse of the world to others. Kaleidoscopes resemble paper towel tubes. One end of the tube has an eyepiece. The other end contains bits of colored glass between two pieces of glass. Two rectangular mirrors reflect the bits of glass multiple times, creating a complicated pattern.

13. What was the author's purpose in writing this selection? _____

_____

14. How does knowing information about when kaleidoscopes were invented contribute to the author's purpose? _____

_____

_____

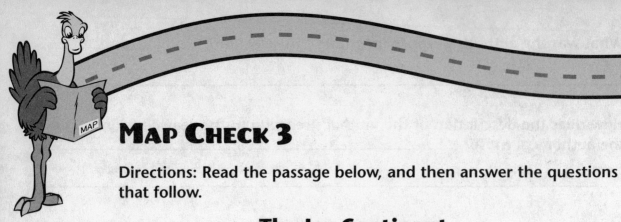

MAP CHECK 3

Directions: Read the passage below, and then answer the questions that follow.

The Icy Continent

1   The continent of Antarctica is located at the South Pole of our planet. Antarctica is a continent of extremes. Snow and ice cover the landmass, even though very little snow falls every year. For six months of the year, the sun shines all day long, but it's still very cold. That is because the wind can blow up to 200 miles per hour. During the other six months of the year, the night never ends.

2   Even though Antarctica is equal to the size of the United States and Mexico combined, very few people live on the icy continent. Why? How would you like to live in a place where the average temperature is –49˚ Celsius? The weather is so harsh that it's often too cold for snow.

3   While it doesn't snow often in Antarctica, there sure is a lot of ice. In some places, the ice that covers Antarctica is two miles thick. That's a lot of ice cubes! In fact, 70 percent of the world's fresh water is frozen in the continent. If Antarctica's ice were chopped and divided, every individual would receive a chunk as big as the Great Pyramid.

4   Life is tranquil for the people who live on Antarctica. The continent has no history of war, and the land belongs to everyone. That means you don't need a passport or a visa to visit. During the winter, only twenty-eight people live in Antarctica. They can't leave during the winter, so they have to use the phone, Internet, and radio to communicate.

5   Scientists watch Antarctica carefully because of its effects on sea level. The ocean has risen about four to eight inches since 1900. If global warming continues, scientists believe that some of Antarctica's ice will melt. This will cause sea levels to rise about three feet over the next hundred years.

6   While this would be a significant increase, scientists are more concerned by what would happen if global warming caused large chunks of ice to break off from the continent. If this occurred, the giant pieces of ice would displace great quantities of water in the ocean. This would cause sea levels to rise by as much as eighteen feet. Many cities could flood.

7   It's difficult to predict whether this will happen. According to scientists, another possibility is that global warming would cause more snow to fall in Antarctica. This would cause a drop in sea levels as moisture was turned into ice.

8   One thing can be certain: Antarctica will continue to draw scientists and tourists to its arctic environment. Despite its harsh conditions, it is a fascinating continent.

1 Paragraph 4 answers which question?

○ **A** What is the average temperature in Antarctica?

○ **B** What is the population of Antarctica during the winter?

○ **C** Where is the continent of Antarctica located?

○ **D** How is global warming affecting Antarctica?

2 Paragraph 6 provides an answer to which question below?

○ **F** Why do scientists worry about the effects of global warming?

○ **G** How many cities would be destroyed if sea levels rose?

○ **H** When do scientists believe chunks of ice will break off Antarctica?

○ **J** How much will the ocean rise over the next hundred years?

3 Paragraph 1 answers which question below?

○ **A** What would cause ocean levels to decrease?

○ **B** Which country owns the cold, icy continent?

○ **C** How fast can the wind blow on the continent?

○ **D** Why do scientists study Antarctica?

4 All of the details below about Antarctica create a sense of how extreme it is *except* for which one?

○ **F** Antarctica has endless night for six months every year.

○ **G** People who live on Antarctica use the phone to communicate.

○ **H** The weather is usually too cold for it to snow.

○ **J** The ice covering the continent is up to two miles thick.

5 According to the passage, the *best* way to describe people who live on Antarctica during the winter is as —

○ **A** hardworking

○ **B** depressed and moody

○ **C** extremely social

○ **D** very isolated

6 The author helps the reader understand how much ice is found in Antarctica by —

○ **F** providing a scientific explanation of how the ice built up on the continent

○ **G** explaining why it is too cold for it to snow very much on the continent

○ **H** stating that global warming could be very dangerous to coastal cities

○ **J** figuring out how much ice every person could get if it were cut into pieces

Directions: Read the passage below, and then answer the questions that follow.

Lost Treasures

1   Treasure maps never fail to ignite the imagination. Left behind by pirates, prospectors, and explorers, these maps offer the promise of leading people to hidden treasures. More often than not, however, treasure maps lead people to dead ends.

2   Captain William Kidd, a famous eighteenth-century pirate, offered British officials his treasure map if they would agree to allow him to live. They refused his offer, and since then, hundreds of people have searched, without luck, for Kidd's loot. Treasure hunters report that the treasure may be located in Canada, New York, or the Caribbean. It may not exist at all.

3   Another famous treasure map was supposed to lead to a rich gold mine in Arizona. According to the tale, two German men saved a Mexican man from a saloon fight in the 1860s. To thank them, the Mexican man led the two to the gold mine. For years, one of the Germans withdrew gold from it and killed anyone who ventured too close. As he was dying, he admitted to the murders and sketched a map, showing people how to reach the mine. Since then, many people have searched in vain for the hidden gold high in the Superstition Mountains near Phoenix. Does the mine really exist?

4   As long as treasure maps exist, treasure hunters will roam the world, following ancient directions of questionable origins. "There's no getting away from a treasure that once fastens upon your mind," said the author Joseph Conrad.

5   This is certainly true of the treasure left behind by a Scottish captain named William Thompson. In the mid-nineteenth century, he made off with tons of gold, jewels, and other valuables from Peru and hid them on Cocos Island, off the coast of Costa Rica. He never returned for the treasure. Before he died, however, he gave his treasure map to a good friend named John Keating. Keating reportedly brought home part of the treasure. Since then, hundreds of others have searched and returned empty-handed. There's speculation that a flood or rockslide changed the landscape of the island and made Thompson's map inaccurate.

6   Is Thomspon's treasure still hidden on the island? Perhaps, but we'll never be entirely sure. In 1978, Costa Rican officials banned all further treasure hunting on the island. Are you curious? Maybe you will become the next famous treasure hunter.

Tip

Before you begin reading a passage, you should always read the title first. That way you can predict what the passage will be about.

7 The author *most likely* wrote the last line of article in order to —

○ **A** warn the reader against believing in hidden treasures

○ **B** show that it's useless to follow treasure maps

○ **C** entice the reader to search for a hidden treasure

○ **D** understand why people make treasure maps

8 Paragraph 5 answers which question below?

○ **F** Where are the Superstition Mountains?

○ **G** What did Joseph Conrad say about treasures?

○ **H** To whom did William Thompson give his map?

○ **J** Why did Captain Kidd offer his treasure map to British officials?

9 The author's purpose in writing paragraph 3 was to —

○ **A** provide detailed directions to a valuable treasure

○ **B** introduce a famous treasure hunter who succeeded

○ **C** make the readers check out a book by Joseph Conrad

○ **D** explain the effect that a treasure can have on people

10 Which of the sentences would *best* complete paragraph 3?

○ **F** It's a mystery that is still unsolved.

○ **G** Sea captains are foolish to hide their riches.

○ **H** Perhaps Thompson's treasure never existed.

○ **J** You should travel to Canada to see it.

11 From the information contained in this article, you can conclude that —

○ **A** Costa Rican officials found the Cocos Island treasure

○ **B** Joseph Conrad bought a treasure map

○ **C** Captain William Kidd was put to death

○ **D** all treasure hunters are violent people

12 What is the author's purpose in asking so many questions in this article?

○ **F** The author doesn't want the reader to know the answers.

○ **G** It helps draw the reader into the article.

○ **H** Questions are a good way of finding out information.

○ **J** Treasure maps often include many riddles in the form of questions.

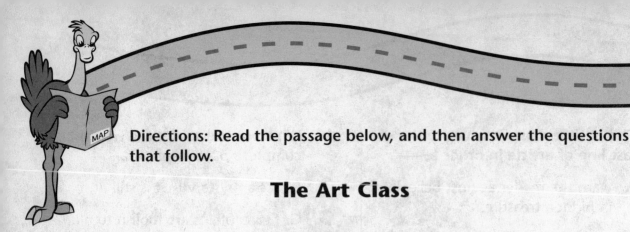

Directions: Read the passage below, and then answer the questions that follow.

The Art Class

1 Terry tossed the baseball to his friend Alexis. "Are you excited for the first day of middle school?" Alexis asked him. "I can't believe it's finally here."

2 "I don't know," Terry said as he caught the ball in his baseball mitt. "I'm sort of worried about taking art."

3 Alexis snorted. "You've got to be kidding. Art is going to be a piece of cake."

4 "For you, maybe," Terry said. "But I can't draw; I can't paint. I'm only good at math and science."

5 When the next morning rolled around, Terry had butterflies in his stomach. He was excited about starting middle school, but he also didn't want to go to art class. Art was his first period. He imagined a class of strange people laughing at him for spilling paint and his mother's upset face when he got a bad grade.

6 Later in art class, Mr. Lythgoe explained his goals to the students. "I want you to get in touch with your creativity. It doesn't matter if you've never picked up a brush before. We all need to express ourselves." Mr. Lythgoe put on a classical CD and told the students to move their colored pencils to the music.

7 Terry glanced around at the other students. They all wore serious expressions and were drawing beautiful things. When he looked at his piece of paper, he only saw scribbles.

8 Mr. Lythgoe turned off the music and approached Terry. "Can you explain your drawing to the class?" he asked.

9 "Umm," Terry muttered. "Can you ask someone else? I'm terrible in art."

10 "Nonsense," Mr. Lythgoe replied. "You've just got to look closely at your drawing."

11 Terry felt his pulse quicken. He stared at the scribbles. The lines didn't seem to make any sense. They looked like nervous doodles. "Well," he started. He had to say something. Everyone was staring at him. "I guess I drew what I felt. The picture shows the crazy brain waves of a confused artist. The lines want to jump off the page, just like I want to run out of the art room."

12 All the other students started laughing. Terry was afraid that Mr. Lythgoe was going to think he was acting smart. Instead, his new art teacher smiled and nodded his head. "That's fantastic," the teacher said. "You've shown how art can express how you're feeling. But I hope by the end of the year you'll feel more at ease in this classroom."

13 Terry smiled and relaxed. He still didn't love art, but he would try.

13 The first paragraph of the story will *most likely* help the reader —

○ **A** find out that Terry and Alexis are next-door neighbors

○ **B** understand Mr. Lythgoe's philosophy about art

○ **C** conclude that Terry is nervous about taking art

○ **D** know that Terry and Alexis are starting a new school

14 Paragraph 5 does *not* answer which question below?

○ **F** Why was Terry feeling nervous about starting school?

○ **G** What was Terry's first class of the day?

○ **H** How did Terry think he would embarrass himself?

○ **J** What caused Terry to dislike drawing so much?

15 Which sentence below would be the *best* one for the author to use at the end of paragraph 6?

○ **A** Terry didn't know what to draw.

○ **B** Studies show that boys are less artistic than girls.

○ **C** Terry felt like art wouldn't be so bad.

○ **D** Art is mandatory in middle school.

16 The author's purpose in writing the story about Terry is to —

○ **F** show why art is the least important subject in school

○ **G** show the importance of trying new things

○ **H** explain how you can develop your musical ability

○ **J** relate a sad story about a boy's first day of school

17 The author *probably* included the final paragraph for the purpose of —

○ **A** proving that people have a hard time changing

○ **B** making the reader feel sad at the end

○ **C** describing how Terry looked when he felt upset

○ **D** showing that Terry felt more comfortable about taking art

18 The author wrote the phrase "Terry had butterflies in his stomach as he got dressed" *probably* to make the reader —

○ **F** understand how Terry was feeling

○ **G** laugh at Terry's foolish worries

○ **H** see the drawing that Terry later made

○ **J** learn how people get sick

MILE 12: PLOT, SETTING, CHARACTERS, AND THEME

Directions: Read the following story and answer the questions that follow.

Henrietta the Cow

1   When Juan first set eyes on Henrietta, she was wobbling unsteadily and calling desperately for her mother. Then, Henrietta was no bigger than a dog. Now, she weighed over five hundred pounds.

2   Juan looked at her proudly. Tomorrow Henrietta would compete in the livestock competition at the county fair. Juan's eyes traveled around the barn on the fairgrounds, looking at the other animals. There were more than a dozen other cows, but none looked as beautiful as Henrietta. Her black and white spotted coat was shiny. Her brown eyes looked calm and cheerful. Her tail swished back and forth, beating a happy tune.

3   "You're going to be a star," Juan whispered in Henrietta's ear.

4   Juan had spent more than a year grooming Henrietta for competition. When she was a calf, he fed her milk from a bottle. Juan could still remember the first time Henrietta had licked his arm. Her bright pink tongue felt like sandpaper.

5   Juan took out a brush and began grooming Henrietta. Barns at the fair were always interesting. Next to the cows, there was a row of pigs. On the other side, there were hutches of funny looking rabbits with long, floppy ears. After cows, Juan's favorite animals were chickens. Juan liked animals like cows and chickens because you could keep them for pets, and they gave you food.

6   Henrietta was strong and obedient. Juan had taught her to follow him. When Juan pulled the rope left, she turned left. When he pulled the rope right, she turned right. It was sometimes difficult to persuade her to begin moving; Juan made a clicking sound with his tongue and cooed, "Let's go Henrietta, let's go."

7   Juan was hoping that Henrietta would be in a good mood tomorrow. "You're going to be very cooperative, aren't you?" Juan whispered. "You're not going to give me any trouble."

8   The judges would rate Henrietta based on her weight, general appearance, and training. Juan checked Henrietta's hooves to make sure they were clean.

9   "That's a pretty nice cow you've got," said Tela, a girl about the same age as Juan. She had braids in her hair, and she smiled at Henrietta.

10   "Thanks," Juan said. "Are you showing an animal?"

11   "No, I'm just here looking around," Tela answered. "My family lives in town, so we don't have room for animals. Did you raise her yourself?"

12   "Yep," Juan answered proudly. "I've been taking care of Henrietta since she was just six weeks old."

13   Henrietta heard her name and mooed. The girl laughed. "It sounds like you've trained her well."

14   Juan flushed with pride. Henrietta was a good cow. He ruffled the hair on her black nose. "She's a great cow," he answered. Suddenly, he was sure that Henrietta would do a terrific job in tomorrow's competition.

1. **Who are two human characters in this story? Identify each character and write an adjective that best describes him or her.**

<u>Character:</u>   <u>Description:</u>

_____   _____

_____   _____

2. **Where does the story mainly take place?** _____

_____

3. **When does the story take place?** _____

_____

4. **What is the main conflict in this story?** _____

_____

_____

_____

5. **How is this conflict resolved?** _____

_____

_____

_____

6. **What is the theme of the story?** _____

_____

_____

_____

MILE 13: GETTING INSIDE A CHARACTER'S HEAD

Have you ever tried to see something from a friend's point of view? Perhaps you wanted to understand why your friend was angry, sad, or happy. You can do this with characters in stories, too. Read the passage carefully and pay attention to clues. As you read try to answer the following questions: How does the character look? How does he or she talk? How does he or she move? How does the character react to different situations?

Directions: Read the story and answer the questions that follow.

The Slippers

1   Once upon a time in ancient Egypt, there lived a wealthy merchant named Charaxos. One day, he was strolling through the market when he noticed a crowd gathering near the place where slaves were sold. He fought his way into the middle of the crowd where he saw a beautiful girl being set upon a stand to be sold.

2   Like Charaxos, she was Greek. Her skin was the color of marble, and her hair was as black as a raven. She was petite, with dainty hands and small feet no bigger than a doll's. Her beauty hypnotized Charaxos. Charaxos decided that moment that he would buy her. Because he was the wealthiest merchant in the area, he quickly accomplished his goal.

3   The walk home was awkward at first. Charaxos, after all, had just purchased her life, and the girl knew nothing about his character. "Tell me your name, my dear girl," Charaxos asked.

4   "I am Rhodopis," the girl answered in a voice more pure than spring water. "I was stolen from home by pirates and sold to a wealthy man who lived on the island of Samos. On the island, a small, ugly man named Aesop adopted me and kept me in a prison."

5   Charaxos tightened his fists when he heard how she had been mistreated. "Go on," he gently urged.

6   "Aesop tried to sweeten the bitter pill of captivity by telling me enchanting stories about animals and human beings. If it were not for his fables, I would not have survived my cruel fate."

7   Charaxos raised his eyebrows.

8   "When I had grown older, my master decided to sell me. That's how I ended up at today's market. I would weep, but I remember Aesop's stories about the importance of remaining strong." Rhodopis's eyes were glistening, but she bit her lip to keep tears from spilling from her eyes.

9   Charaxos felt his heart swell. What a brave and heroic girl! There was nothing he wouldn't do for her. In fact, he decided then that he would treat Rhodopis like a daughter.

10 As soon as they reached Charaxos's compound, he sent his servants scurrying to prepare a room for Rhodopis. Within a week, merchants of jewels and clothing had made many visits to the house, and carpenters had come, carrying lumber and slinging tools, and gone, leaving behind a house. The gardener hauled in loads of rosebushes, tulip bulbs, and strawberry plants, so that when Rhodopis stepped out the front door of her new house in her beautiful clothing she was greeted by the sweet scent of roses and strawberries.

11 When she smiled, Charaxos felt like his heart might melt.

12 One day as Charaxos was totaling his balance sheets, Rhodopis was swimming in the pool in her garden. The sun shone brightly overhead, and it was another hot summer day in Egypt. Only one solitary cloud swam lazily across the sky. Suddenly, however, Rhodopis noticed an eagle diving straight toward the pool. Rhodopis's servants shrieked and dove into the bushes, and Rhodopis froze in the pool. The eagle swooped down and plucked Rhodopis's rose-colored slipper from the edge of the pool, and then climbed back into the sky and vanished.

13 The sound of Rhodopis's weeping made Charaxos rise from his chair and run to the edge of the garden. "What is wrong?" he called out. "What is wrong?"

14 When Rhodopis told Charaxos about the eagle, he shook his head, wiped the tears from her cheeks, and sent a servant to buy new shoes immediately.

15 Life returned to normal. Rhodopis swam in the afternoons, and Charaxos attended to his business so that he could shower more gifts on his adopted daughter. Neither of them knew that the eagle had flown to the courtyard of the pharaoh, Amasis, and dropped the slipper in the pharaoh's lap. The ruler looked closely at the red slipper, admiring its excellent workmanship and tiny size. He felt sure that the woman who had lost it was lovely beyond belief.

16 The pharaoh issued a decree, announcing that the woman whose foot fit the tiny shoe would become his bride, and he sent out his messengers to deliver it.

17 News of Rhodopis's beauty spread like fire through the kingdom. Messengers heard about the beautiful Greek girl living in the house of Charaxos and found the girl in her favorite place beside the pool. When they presented her with the shoe, she cried out. She had thought the shoe was lost forever. And when the messenger saw how easily it fit her foot, they wanted to take her to the Pharaoh immediately. The messenger also informed Rhodopis that the pharaoh wanted to marry the woman whose foot fit the shoe. Rhodopis was overcome by the news of her good fortune, and she agreed to marry the pharaoh.

18 Charaxos was saddened that his adopted daughter would leave the house. He paced back and forth in the garden. His stomach churned, and his heart seemed to be shriveling. When Rhodopis swept out of the house, looking more radiant than ever, Charaxos swallowed the lump in his throat and embraced her. Through happy tears, he whispered in her ear, "You are getting what you deserve, my dear. You are getting what you deserve."

1. How does Charaxos feel when he first sees Rhodopis?

    _____

    _____

    _____

2. Write a sentence from the story that supports your answer.

    _____

    _____

3. After Charaxos hears the tale of Rhodopis's childhood, how does he feel?

    _____

    _____

    _____

4. Write a sentence from the story that supports your answer.

    _____

    _____

5. How does Charaxos feel when Rhodopis finds out that the pharaoh wants to marry her?

    _____

    _____

    _____

6. Write a sentence from the story that supports your answer.

    _____

    _____

Directions: Choose three adjectives from the box that best describe Charaxos, the main character of the story. Write each adjective in the box at the top of each column below. In each column, list what Charaxos says or does in the story that tells you he could be described by this adjective.

Generous	Angry
Cold-hearted	Envious
Ambitious	Lazy
Sad	

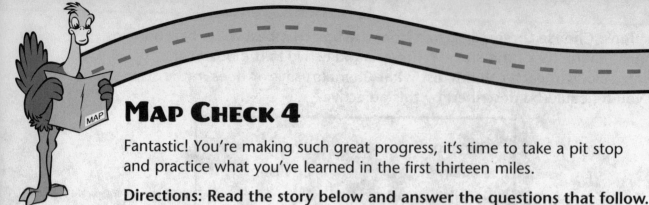

MAP CHECK 4

Fantastic! You're making such great progress, it's time to take a pit stop and practice what you've learned in the first thirteen miles.

Directions: Read the story below and answer the questions that follow.

On a Hike

1 We walked in a silent single file, like a snake. Fear kept us quiet. Overhead, thunder roared and distant lightning brightened the sky. We were above the tree line, exposed, and we knew we had to hike down quickly. Our boots were ankle-deep in mud. Suddenly, a bolt of lightning split the sky in two. My hands tingled with electricity.

2 "Keep moving," one of our group leaders called.

3 There was more silence. If one person cried, we would all start crying. It was raining harder now. The drops felt like the tips of pins against my cheek. I shivered. My fingers were becoming numb.

4 "Jamie," I said, "do you think we're going to make it down?"

5 Jamie didn't answer. I turned to the person walking behind me.

6 "Beatrice, what's going to happen to us?" I asked. Beatrice was the oldest student in the group.

7 "Keep going," she answered. "And watch where you walk. It's slippery, but we need to get down fast."

8 This was hardly the answer I was expecting. I wanted someone to reassure me that we would get back safely. I stopped in the middle of the trail and crossed my arms.

9 "What do you think you're doing?" Beatrice hissed.

10 "I'm not taking another step," I answered. "Why did we come on this stupid hike in the first place?" I could feel tears welling up in my eyes.

11 Another wave of thunder rumbled, and a bolt of lightning cracked above us. Beatrice grabbed my arm and pushed me forward. "This isn't the time for talking," she said, "or for feeling scared. Just think about how each step is bringing you closer to taking a nice hot shower."

12 We sloshed down the mountain through a stream that hours earlier had been a dry trail. Several times, I almost gave up and sat down, but then I remembered what Beatrice said. I repeated, "hot shower, hot shower." Sometimes, I added, "chocolate bar, chocolate bar."

13 Finally, after what seemed like hours, we reached the trees. And then, all of a sudden, the storm ended. The sun burned through the clouds, and steam rose from the ground. It was strange how quickly things changed. Now it was delightfully hot! Instead of thinking about a hot shower, I began dreaming about taking a dip in the lake near where we were staying!

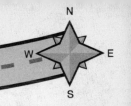

1 How did the narrator feel when Beatrice told her they needed to walk fast?

○ **A** Motivated

○ **B** Content

○ **C** Upset

○ **D** Surprised

2 The *best* description of Beatrice is as —

○ **F** determined

○ **G** harsh

○ **H** selfish

○ **J** easygoing

3 At the end of the story, the *best* description of the narrator is as —

○ **A** incredibly stubborn

○ **B** very cold

○ **C** surprised and happy

○ **D** extremely ungrateful

4 At the beginning of the story, what is the *best* description of how the group feels?

○ **F** Tired but chatty

○ **G** Panicked and scared

○ **H** Cautious and slow

○ **J** Silent and thoughtful

5 From this story, you can infer that —

○ **A** the group is in danger of getting lost

○ **B** it's good to eat chocolate when you're hiking

○ **C** the group leaders are older than the others

○ **D** the narrator is grateful to have Beatrice around

6 Upon seeing a bolt of lightning, the narrator felt —

○ **F** irritated that Beatrice had so much energy

○ **G** excited to be on a hike

○ **H** like taking a dip in the lake

○ **J** cold and terrified of the weather

Use clues to get inside a character's head. Clues can include things like how the character says things, how the character responds to different situations, and even how the character moves!

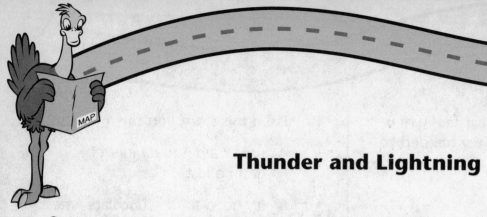

Thunder and Lightning

1 Once upon a time, there lived a beautiful young woman who had two sons, Amitai and Anil. Her husband was a cloud, and he lived far away in the sky. One day the boys asked about their father.

2 Their mother stared into the distance. The sun was setting, and there was single cloud in the sky. "That is your father," she answered.

3 The boys' eyes opened wide in amazement. "Can we visit him?"

4 "Yes," their mother answered. "You may visit him, but you must make your journey without stopping. First, you must get by Wind, who is your father's oldest brother. He may try to blow you away and prevent you from visiting your father. You must be strong against him."

5 The beautiful young woman blinked away her tears when her brave boys set off on their journey. They had never been separated before, but she knew her children would want to see their father someday.

6 The boys traveled for many days across the plains and slowly climbed the great mountain in the east. Wind tried to blow them back, but they wrapped their arms around a tree, closed their eyes, and prayed for the storm to end. Wind exhaled another long breath of air. He loved to see people suffer. Finally, he got tired, and the boys continued on their way. The younger boy, Anil, often stopped and doubted they would ever reach the clouds. Amitai always pushed him forward.

7 The boys climbed higher up the mountain. At times, they couldn't see their way because their vision was obscured by Mist, the younger cousin of Cloud. Amitai took his brother's hand and led him through the blanket of whiteness. Even though he sometimes trembled for fear of getting lost, he walked with great assurance.

8 In the mornings, the sun was brightly shining, and the boys' hearts felt heavy. The sun drove their father into hiding, and the boys feared he would never reappear.

9 Finally, near the top of the mountain where nothing grew, they woke one morning in the middle of a cloud.

10 "Cloud," called one of the boys. "Is that you, Father? Is it us, your sons."

11 "I am Cloud," boomed a loud voice. "I will recognize you as my sons if you can prove it by doing what I do."

12 Amitai sent a streak of lightning across the sky and then Anil rumbled like thunder.

13 "Do it again!" Cloud ordered.

14 The boys filled the sky with daggers of lightning and ear-splitting thunder, and the people living in the valley shuddered to see such a storm. Because Cloud has such a poor memory, his sons must prove they are his sons by producing both thunder and lightning whenever they visit him.

7 In order to be recognized as Cloud's sons, the two boys had to —

○ **A** produce thunder and lightning

○ **B** make an important sacrifice

○ **C** climb a tall mountain

○ **D** stare into the distance

8 How did Anil feel during the journey?

○ **F** Optimistic

○ **G** Happy

○ **H** Discouraged

○ **J** Amused

9 Based on the story, Wind is *best* described as —

○ **A** thoughtful

○ **B** cruel

○ **C** talkative

○ **D** kind

10 Which of the following descriptions fits *best* for Amitai?

○ **F** Brave and caring

○ **G** Never fearful

○ **H** Scared and hungry

○ **J** Very lazy

11 How does the boys' mother feel when they leave to find their father?

○ **A** Glad and joyful

○ **B** Irritated and bitter

○ **C** Sad but accepting

○ **D** Unhappy but relieved

12 Based on the information in this myth, you can conclude that —

○ **F** Amitai is younger than Anil

○ **G** Cloud lives on the west side of the mountain

○ **H** Mist and Wind are part of the same family

○ **J** the older brother can never return home

Directions: Read the following poem, and then answer the questions that follow.

Grandpa

1   My Grandpa died the other night
2   But he didn't go without a fight
3   Born premature, in nineteen twenty-two
4   His parents didn't know what to do

5   Orphaned when he was a little lad
6   At times his life was really sad
7   Asthma made it hard to breathe
8   So chilly weather made him wheeze

9   He rode back and forth to school by horse
10   Earned money on a ranch of course
11   He went to college by pumping gas
12   And graduated at the top of his class

13   Out of sight, but still in my mind
14   I think of places where we dined
15   Grandma Ruth and Daughter Sue
16   Grandkids, cousins, and brothers too

17   Out of sight, but still in my head
18   I think of the life he led
19   A cowboy in a cowboy town
20   And how he rode motorcyles 'round

21   Out of sight, but still in my heart
22   I think of what he made me start
23   Writing stories to make him laugh
24   Trying to follow his humorous path

25   Out of sight, but still in my core
26   I remember the smile he always wore
27   The jokes he told, the songs he belted
28   The children whose frowns he melted

29   Out of sight, but still part of me
30   In everything I do and see
31   In every step in leather boots
32   I'm connected to my Grandpa's roots

13 In the poem, Grandpa's childhood might be *best* characterized as —

○ **A** difficult

○ **B** comforting

○ **C** delightful

○ **D** interesting

14 Grandpa's life began with difficulty because he was —

○ **F** born premature

○ **G** taken to the hospital

○ **H** given up on

○ **J** earning money on a ranch

15 How does the narrator feel about Grandpa between lines 29–32 of the poem?

○ **A** Jealous

○ **B** Terrified

○ **C** Impressed

○ **D** Emotional

16 The narrator of the poem might be *best* characterized as —

○ **F** grateful

○ **G** amused

○ **H** sad

○ **J** rebellious

17 The *best* description of Grandpa is as —

○ **A** sad and depressed

○ **B** irresponsible

○ **C** adventurous and funny

○ **D** very bitter

18 After reading this poem, you can conclude that —

○ **F** Grandpa had three of his own children

○ **G** all children used to ride horses to school

○ **H** Grandpa studied writing in college

○ **J** asthma worsens in cold weather

MILE 14: METAPHOR, SIMILE, AND PERSONIFICATION

To do well in your fifth-grade reading class (and on the SOL Reading/Literature and Research test), you should be able to identify and analyze figurative language. That includes being able to recognize a metaphor, a simile, and personification, which all make comparisons between two different things. These terms might sound complicated, but they're not. Once you know what they are, it's easy to understand how they're used.

I am a rock; I am an island: **Metaphor.**

After it rains, the pond is like an ocean: **Simile.**

The wind whispered in the darkness: **Personification.**

Directions: Write the terms listed in the box below next to the correct definitions.

Metaphor

Simile

Personification

1. a comparison between two different things that is formed with "like," "as," or "than"_____

2. a comparison between two things that is usually formed with a "to be" verb

_____

3. a figure of speech that gives animals, ideas, or objects human qualities and

characteristics _____

Directions: Read the sentences below and decide what type of figurative language is being used in each sentence. Using the three terms from the box on the last page, write the correct type on the line next to each sentence. You may use the terms in the box more than once.

1. She turned as red as a beet after the teacher took the note she was writing and read it aloud to the whole class. _____

2. The cat jumped for joy when I finally returned from my vacation.

   _____

3. The moon is a spotlight, lighting up the woods around the cabin.

   _____

4. The tired, old truck gasped for air before chugging up the hill.

   _____

5. He snorted like a pig before stuffing more lemon meringue pie in his face.

   _____

6. Our house cried, "Don't leave," as we loaded the final box into the moving van and locked the front door for the last time. _____

7. Lollipop bushes and green coconut grass made the house look very inviting.

   _____

8. She was an elephant on the basketball court: slow and clumsy, but strong.

   _____

9. In the distance, the mountains looked like daggers. _____

10. The trees shook their fists at the gray, angry skies. _____

Directions: Read the six passages over the next two pages. After each passage, answer the questions that follow.

When my mother gets mad, you'd better watch out! She is as <u>ferocious as a tiger</u>. She prowls around the house, ready to pounce on the first person to cross her path or leave a dirty dish on the counter. Whenever she goes into one of her tiger phases, I make sure to head outside to play with my friends.

11. **What kind of figurative language is used in the underlined selection?**

_____

12. **What does the underlined selection mean?** _____

_____

<u>The house let out a long sigh of defeat</u> as Hai Jin and her family closed the door behind them. There was a For Sale in the front yard. "It seems sort of sad to leave," Hai Jin said. "We've lived here our whole lives."

Hai Jin's mother had a gleam in her eye. "It's not sad at all," she answered. "Our new house has a swimming pool. You'll forget this old house in no time."

13. **What kind of figurative language is used in the underlined selection?**

_____

14. **What does the underlined selection mean?** _____

_____

The photographer, Walfredo, paced back and forth in the studio. "<u>You are the sun</u>!" he cried to his model. "I want you to shine for me. I want you to look positively radiant for these photographs."

The young woman posing on the stage smiled and tossed her hair. The camera clicked.

15. **What kind of figurative language is used in the underlined selection?**

_____

16. **What does the underlined selection mean?** _____

_____

The sun shone brightly overhead. The waves lapped lazily against the beach.
<u>The seagulls were like noisy children</u>, laughing loudly and for no apparent reason.
Cassandra and her three sisters covered themselves in sunscreen and propped up
their giant beach umbrellas. It was going to be another hot day, but what did it
matter? They had nothing to do but read their books, nap, dip in the ocean, and
sip cool sodas. They were on holiday.

17.   **What kind of figurative language is used in the underlined selection?**

_____

18.   **What does the underlined selection mean?** _____

_____

When Edu woke and saw the ground was covered in snow, he smiled widely.
"School's cancelled," the radio announced. <u>The day was a beautifully wrapped
present</u>. When Edu had gone to sleep, the night had been cold with no sign of
the coming storm. He snuggled underneath his comforter and tried to decide
what to do. He could spend the day building snow forts and snowmen, or he
could stay inside and paint. He'd never painted a picture of the snow before.
He wondered whether it would be difficult.

19.   **What kind of figurative language is used in the underlined selection?**

_____

20.   **What does the underlined selection mean?** _____

_____

The weather on the night of the hike was cool and crisp. It was perfect for staring
up at the sky at the millions of stars. Unfortunately, our camp counselor wouldn't
let us rest until we got to the cabin. <u>The moon smiled at us as we walked in its
dim light</u>. Owls hooted in the distance. It was a really enjoyable hike, and the
nature trail helped us to realize just how beautiful the woods around us were.

21.   **What kind of figurative language is used in the underlined selection?**

_____

22.   **What does the underlined selection mean?** _____

_____

MILE 15: MOOD

You've probably noticed how movies can change your mood. Some movies excite you, others make you laugh, and others make you cry. Stories, poems, and other reading selections also can make you feel things.

The mood describes the overall feeling of a passage. Determining mood is much like drawing conclusions. You use context clues, like figurative language, in the passage to help you. Pay attention to the way the scene is described and how characters speak and move.

Directions: Read the following passages. Then choose an adjective from the box below that best describes the mood of each and write it next to the passage. Circle the figure of speech and underline the figurative language in the passage.

Serious	Nonsensical
Humorous	Mysterious
Joyful	Sorrowful

The old woman cackled like a hen and shuffled down the stairs. The basement was pitch black and smelled like a swamp. "I'm coming," the woman cried.

The woman snapped on a light dangling from a wire. The basement was empty except for a giant box and next to it, a rocking chair. The woman knocked on the box. "Hello," she called. "Are you sleeping or are you awake?"

1.   Mood: _____

2.   **Figure of Speech:**   Simile   Metaphor   Personification

Eliza Elizabeth was an elegant dandelion. No one liked her, and yet she attended all of the balls, dressed up in a yellow dress that was so bright that it nearly blinded everyone.

The other women tried to poison Eliza by whispering nasty things about her, but it never worked. Eliza would hear their cruel words, toss her yellow hair, and plant herself next to another dance partner.

3.   Mood: _____

4.   **Figure of Speech:**   Simile   Metaphor   Personification

Matt knocked on the principal's door and then slowly entered. He stood up straight with his hands in his pockets, took a deep breath, and swallowed. "I have something to confess," he said. "I pulled the fire alarm."

The principal's face darkened suddenly like a storm sweeping across a sky. "Why on earth did you do that, young man?"

5.   **Mood:** _____

6.   **Figure of Speech:**   Simile   Metaphor   Personification

"Today is upside-down day," Lucy cried, putting her boots on her ears and her wool cap on her feet. "Good night, Mother."

Her father looked confused. "It's morning still, and I'm your father."

Lucy began walking around the living room backwards. She told him, "Don't be as sharp as a butter knife." Out the window, the sun was shining. "Look out the window. You can't see anything because it's pitch black."

7.   **Mood:** _____

8.   **Figure of Speech:**   Simile   Metaphor   Personification

The yellow Labrador retriever looked around the playground, inspecting the other dogs, sniffed, then cast his sad eyes down toward the ground. His owner was nowhere to be found.

Just minutes before, he had been running around with a chocolate Labrador. His owner was standing next to the drinking fountain watching him. Then, he looked away and his owner disappeared. The yellow Labrador flopped down on the ground and began to whimper. He was hungry, and he wanted to go home.

9.   **Mood:** _____

10.   **Figure of Speech:**   Simile   Metaphor   Personification

Mile 16: Elements of Poetry

To analyze poetry, you need to become familiar with different elements of poetry. Once you've learned the definitions below, you'll use them to figure out the overall mood of a poem.

Directions: Write the terms from the box next to their definitions listed below. Then read the poem on the next page and answer the questions that follow it.

Mood	Rhythm
Theme	Stanza
Rhyme	

1. Words that end with the same sounds _____

2. The way the poem makes you feel _____

3. A grouping of two or more lines of poetry that are about the same length or share a rhyme scheme _____

4. The musical beat of the words _____

5. The author's meaning or the underlying moral _____

Outside in the Weather

1 I'm going dancing in the pouring rain

2 I'll rock to the rhythm of the pitter-patter

3 If I get soaked, it doesn't matter

4 I'm going to groove until the rain goes away

5 I'm going strolling in the drifting snow

6 I'll march through the flurry of the tiny flakes

7 I may catch a chill, but who cares for goodness' sake

8 I'm going to walk until the snow melts away

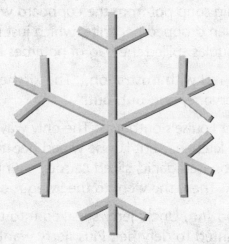

6. **How many stanzas are there in the poem?** _____

7. **How many lines are in each stanza of the poem?** _____

8. **Which lines rhyme in each stanza?** _____

9. **Write an adjective that best describes the mood of the poem.** _____

10. **Write one sentence that best describes the theme of "Outside in the Weather."**

    _____

    _____

MAP CHECK 5

Directions: Read the story below, and then answer the questions that follow.

Birthday Soup

1 Everyone in the family wanted to do something special for Grandma Mabel's birthday. Aunt Louise, Uncle Jerry, Baby Didi, Helen, and Douglas gathered in the living room to discuss the birthday plans. "I think we should make a big pot of soup," Aunt Louise proposed. "Grandma Mabel loves soup, and we can eat it for dinner and tell stories."

2 Everyone agreed and went into the kitchen to begin cooking the soup. Aunt Louise was bending down to get the big soup pot from the cupboard when she bumped into Helen, who was dicing carrots. Helen dropped her knife, which just missed Uncle Jerry's toe. Jerry screamed so loudly that Douglas spilled the bag of potatoes he was carrying.

3 Aunt Louise's face became red with frustration. "The kitchen isn't big enough for all of us," she screamed. "Everyone, out, out, out!"

4 The family was used to Aunt Louise's outbursts. The only way to calm her was by leaving, and they slipped out of the kitchen. Aunt Louise wiped her hands on her apron and began to hum. She diced onions, bruised garlic, sliced carrots, chunked potatoes, and put the ingredients in a pot to cook. Then, she went to the living room for a nap.

5 While Aunt Louise was snoozing, Uncle Jerry sneaked into the kitchen. Aunt Louise was very bossy, and he wanted to defy her. Plus, Jerry wanted to add his own special ingredients to the soup. He lifted the lid and added four dashes of hot sauce, two pinches of sugar, and a whole lemon. Grandma Mabel was going to love the soup.

6 Baby Didi cautiously tiptoed down the hallway and then scampered into the kitchen. Her favorite food was pickles, and she found a jar in the fridge. She dumped every single pickle from the jar into the soup pot.

7 Helen and Douglas had the same idea as the rest of the family. Because she loved dairy products, Helen added three dollops of sour cream and some grated cheddar cheese to the soup. Douglas loved spices and added a pinch of every spice in the spice cabinet. They both slipped back to their rooms to finish wrapping the presents.

8 A potent smell woke Aunt Louise from her nap. At first, she imagined that Uncle Jerry had walked into the living room in his socks—his feet emitted a terrible odor! But after opening her eyes and sniffing the air, she realized the odor was coming from the kitchen. She sprung up from the couch and hurried to the kitchen. After lifting the lid from the pot, she screamed.

9 The odor was like nothing she'd ever smelled—worse than rotting leaves, worse than sour milk, even worse than Jerry's feet.

10 "What have I always said?" Aunt Louise demanded. "You should let me do the cooking."

1 The main idea of this story is that —

○ A soup can be made with many ingredients

○ B bossy people shouldn't be in control

○ C everyone should add whatever he or she wants to the soup

○ D too many cooks can ruin the soup

2 The author's purpose in writing paragraph 2 was *mainly* to —

○ F give the reader a recipe for making special birthday soup

○ G entertain the reader by showing chaos in the kitchen

○ H show the reader why it's important to compromise

○ J help the reader picture the house where the story takes place

3 After reading paragraph 6, the reader will *probably* feel —

○ A proud of Didi

○ B concerned about the soup

○ C hungry and ready to eat

○ D bored and serious

4 In paragraph 8, descriptions such as "worse than rotting leaves" and "worse than sour milk" leave the reader with an idea of the —

○ F tastiness of the soup

○ G depth of Louise's temper

○ H importance of perfume

○ J ruin of the soup

5 Verbs such as "tiptoed," "slipped," and "sneaked" give readers the impression of —

○ A fear

○ B secretiveness

○ C noise

○ D bossiness

6 By the end of the story, how did Aunt Louise feel?

○ F Sleepy

○ G Delighted

○ H Enraged

○ J Hungry

Directions: Read the poem below, and then answer the questions that follow.

Birthday

1 Now the cake
2 We must bake!
3 Blow up balloons
4 Dance to tunes.
5 Friends attend
6 And likewise kin.
7 The room is filled
8 With happiness
9 Happiness, happiness,
      to wish you a happy birthday.

10 Birthday girl
11 With golden curls;
12 Streamers flutter
13 Like her heart.
14 Shouts and cheers
15 For nine big years,
16 Claps and smiles
17 And hugs and kisses
18 Happiness, happiness,
      to wish you a happy birthday.

19 A burning torch
20 Lights the porch;
21 Come and watch
22 Fireworks go off!
23 Let me light
24 Your sparklers white.
25 Let me place it
26 In your small hand.
27 Happiness, happiness,
      we wish you a happy birthday.

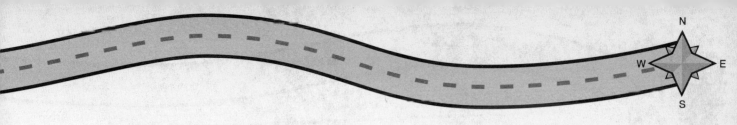

7 What is the *best* description of the girl in the poem?

○ **A** Shy

○ **B** Glum

○ **C** Scared

○ **D** Excited

8 The phrase "streamers flutter like her heart" in lines 15 and 16 in the poem mean that —

○ **F** the birthday girl was very energetic

○ **G** the birthday girl had ribbons pinned to her dress

○ **H** the birthday girl's heart was beating too rapidly

○ **J** the birthday girl was going to fly like a bird

9 This poem is *mainly* about —

○ **A** lighting sparklers for a girl

○ **B** baking cakes for birthdays

○ **C** how much fun birthday parties are

○ **D** setting off fireworks

10 The author *most likely* repeats lines 9 and 10 throughout the poem to make the reader —

○ **F** memorize those lines of the poem

○ **G** feel the joyfulness of birthdays

○ **H** grow bored with the repetition

○ **J** understand that it is a birthday

11 After reading lines 14 through 17, the reader will *probably* feel —

○ **A** excited for the birthday girl

○ **B** disappointed in the party

○ **C** quiet and tired

○ **D** sad for the little girl

12 Descriptions such as "burning," "light," and "sparklers" create in the reader an understanding of the —

○ **F** brightness of the fireworks

○ **G** danger of fire

○ **H** cost of the party

○ **J** excitement of the family

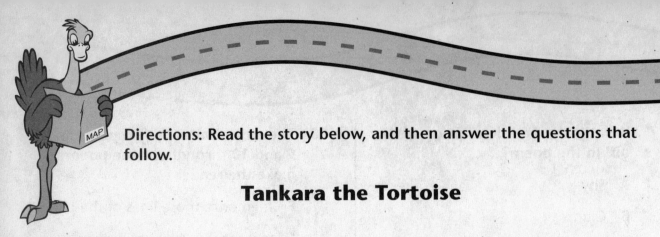

Directions: Read the story below, and then answer the questions that follow.

Tankara the Tortoise

1   Tankara the tortoise had used up all of his salt, and his formerly delicious meals were now bland. He decided to visit his brother and ask him to spare some salt. Tankara's brother had a lot of salt, and he gladly shared his wealth. The only problem was that Tankara had no way to carry the salt home. "I have an idea," his brother proposed. "I will wrap the salt in a piece of cloth and tie it up with a string. Then you can drag the parcel behind you."

2   "A brilliant idea," exclaimed Tankara, and he set off for home, dragging the salt behind him. Tankara's mouth watered as he imagined the tasty food he would cook later that night. His brother was a generous turtle, and thinking this, Tankara hardly noticed the burning of the string across his shell. Suddenly, his parcel of salt snagged on something. Tankara turned around and saw a large lizard sitting on the parcel of salt.

3   "Get off my salt!" he cried. "This is a parcel of seasoning, not a city bus. If you need a ride, hire a horse."

4   The lizard gazed at Tankara lazily and said, "What are you screaming about? I was just walking along when I saw this tasty bag of salt. Since I took it, the salt is now mine."

5   "You are talking nonsense," Tankara said as quickly as a hare. "It is clear who owns this salt. I am holding the string that is attached to the salt. That is proof that it is mine."

6   The lizard refused to budge, insisting that they visit the elders to have their disagreement settled in court. Tankara had no option and he reluctantly walked to the court where a group of wise old men with long beards sat in judgment.

7   The old men listened to Tankara and the lizard and stroked their beards. They decided that the salt should be divided. Since the lizard found the salt in the middle of the road, he could take half of it. Poor Tankara was left with only half the salt, and he left the court with a heavy heart. Although Tankara walked slowly, he quickly devised a plan for payback.

8   The next day he headed for the lizard's house. When Tankara saw the lazy lizard eating a tasty meal of salted ants, he snuck behind him and grabbed his soft, tender belly. "Look what I found," Tankara called out loudly. "I was walking down the path when I found a lizard who belongs to no one."

9   The lizard was perplexed, but Tankara continued: "I think we should take this matter to the elders. Since they decided the salt case so fairly, let them decide this matter as well."

10 With great concern, the elders listened to both sides of the argument. They discussed it in their chambers and returned to issue their ruling. "Since the bag of salt was cut in two," one elder said very gravely, "so too must the lizard be cut in two."

11 Tankara quickly seized a knife while the lizard begged for mercy. Tankara's heart softened, and he only sliced off the lizard's tail, sparing his life. This is why lizards, to this day, lose their tails—from fear of losing their lives.

---

13 Descriptive words such as "lazy," "soft," and "tender" help the reader understand the —

○ A anger of the turtle

○ B taste of the stew

○ C length of the turtle's journey

○ D weakness of the lizard

14 At the very end of the story, how did Tankara feel toward the lizard?

○ F Curious and friendly

○ G Confused and defeated

○ H Furious and vengeful

○ J Angry but merciful

15 After finishing this story, readers can conclude that —

○ A people should be allowed to keep what they find

○ B you should treat others well even if they don't always do the same

○ C lizards are crafty creatures that will do anything to get what they want

○ D turtles are mean creatures that are often vengeful

16 When the author wrote, "Tankara's heart softened," he or she meant that —

○ F Tankara's heart was defective

○ G Tankara's heart was weak from walking

○ H Tankara felt sleepy

○ J Tankara felt bad for the lizard

17 The *best* description of Tankara's brother is as —

○ A delightful

○ B generous

○ C mean

○ D curious

18 The author's purpose in writing paragraph 3 was *most likely* to make the reader —

○ F understand that turtles prefer to use salt when cooking

○ G learn how lizards get from one place to another

○ H realize that animals are able to talk to each other

○ J be amused by the dialogue and want to continue reading

MILE 17: USING CHARTS WITH STORIES

Sometimes making a chart can help you figure out the connections between different ideas or characters in a story.

Directions: Read the following passage. Then use information from the passage to fill in the blank spaces in the chart on the following page.

Webster's Dictionary

1. Noah Webster was a wordy man. He studied law. He taught school. He wrote a spelling book. And he created An American Dictionary of the English Language.

2. Webster was born in the eighteenth century in the state of Connecticut. He attended law school until a family crisis brought him back home, where he taught school to support his family.

3. In those day, teachers didn't just teach. They did everything: They cleaned the school, repaired the roof, taught spelling, drilled arithmetic, and directed plays. Even though Webster wanted only to teach, he did all of the other chores cheerfully to set a good example for his students.

4. Eventually, Webster was able to tackle his first big project: writing the Blue-Backed Speller. During those times, words were spelled every which way, but Webster believed there should be a standard spelling for each word. That's why he wrote the book.

5. Because there weren't big companies to distribute books or giant bookstores where children could buy books, Webster rode his horse throughout the original thirteen states giving away free copies and taking orders from schools. The book was an enormous success, with more than a hundred million copies sold.

6. Webster was also ambitious. Not only did he want people to spell correctly, he wanted them to speak the same language. In those days Americans spoke English so differently from one place to another that they didn't understand each other. Webster thought everyone would live together more peacefully if they spoke one language, or "mother tongue."

7. For more than twenty years, he worked on An American Dictionary of the English Language, journeying around the country and overseas to learn the history of words and how they were first used. He changed the spellings of many words to ensure there were standard ways of writing them. For example, he changed "musick" to "music" and "plough" to "plow." Webster also standardized pronunciations so that everyone spoke the words in the same way.

8. At the end of his years of hard, solitary work, he published a dictionary of 70,000 words. Besides the Bible, it has sold more copies than any other book published in English. It's still around today. Although the Merriam family bought the rights to print the book, if you look around your classroom, you'll probably see at least one dictionary known as the "Merriam-Webster" dictionary.

Noah Webster created two well-known books. Use the four pieces of information in the box below to fill in the spaces of the graphic organizer. Make sure to write the name of the missing book below and fill in the details about the books below the titles.

Standardized spelling for many words	more than 100 million
An American Dictionary of the English Language	Contained standard ways to pronounce words

Noah Webster's Books

Names of the Books

Blue-Backed Speller	• 1._____ _____ _____ _____

Details about the Books

• Webster's first book • 2._____ _____ _____ • 3. Sold _____ copies • Webster delivered it on horseback	• Webster spent more than twenty years writing it • 4._____ _____ _____ • Sold more copies than any English book after the Bible • Contains 70,000 words

MILE 18: USING CHARTS WITH FACTS

You probably read and use charts all the time. You do it every time you look at a bus schedule to figure out when a bus is leaving or read the television guide to find out when your favorite program is on.

Directions: Below is a schedule of trains leaving from Washington, D.C., for cities around the country. Use the schedule to answer the questions.

Destination	Train Number	Departure Time	Arrival Time
Atlanta	789	8:00 A.M.	7:30 P.M.
Boston	345	11:00 A.M.	9:45 P.M.
Chicago	702	4:30 A.M.	6:30 P.M.
Denver	124	4:00 A.M.	8:00 P.M.
New Orleans	451	6:00 A.M.	4:10 P.M.
New York City	903	3:45 A.M.	9:15 A.M.

1. What is the number of the train that leaves earliest in the morning? _____

2. What is the destination of train number 702? _____

3. What time does train number 789 leave for Atlanta? _____

4. What time does train number 451 arrive in New Orleans? _____

5. What is the destination city of the train that leaves latest in the day?

    _____

Directions: Use the information from the box below to fill in the missing information on the chart that follows.

Cat's Meow trail takes 4 hours and is 6.5 miles long.

The most difficult trail has a waterfall along the way.

At the midway point is a one-room schoolhouse that was used in the nineteenth century.

Ann's Peak trail is 9.5 miles long.

Shark Tooth Mountain Recreation Area

There's a hike for everyone in the Shark Tooth Mountain Recreation Area. Use this chart to choose the perfect trail for you. It includes information on the length and difficulty of the hike as well as what you can hope to see along the way.

Trail	Length	Difficulty	Comments
Bollen Valley	3 miles	◓	_____ _____ _____
Cat's Meow	_____	◓	This trail includes the best of Shark Tooth Mountain Recreation Area: great views, waterfalls, and hidden meadows.
Sunflower Meadow	1.2 miles	○	There is a perfect place to picnic on this trail. The granite boulders make nice picnic tables.
_____	9.5 miles	●	Great views of the whole valley. Be prepared to scramble up the last mile.
Three Streams	4 miles	_____	On this trail, you'll see a beautiful waterfall at mile 2.

KEY
○ = Easy
◓ = Intermediate
● = Difficult

MILE 19: READING GRAPHS

A graph shows information through pictures rather than through words. Graphs usually show information that involves numbers. It is often easier to understand this kind of information when it is presented on a graph.

Directions: Below is a pie graph. Use the information on the pie graph to answer the questions that follow.

Ms. Ruiz's Students' Favorite Class

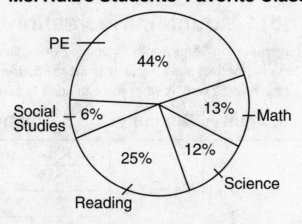

1. Which subject do students like the most?

   _____

2. Which subject do students like the least?

   _____

3. Which subjects do students like about the same?

   _____

4. What percentage of students likes reading?

   _____

5. Do more students like PE, or do more students like math, science, reading, and social studies combined?

   _____

6. How can you answer question #5 without adding up all the numbers?

   _____

Directions: Use the information in the box to fill in the missing information on the bar graph below.

The snack bar sold 16 apples in December.
Eight bags of nuts were sold during December.
The snack bar sold 32 cans of soda in December.

Candy and Snacks Sold: December

Number of Items Sold

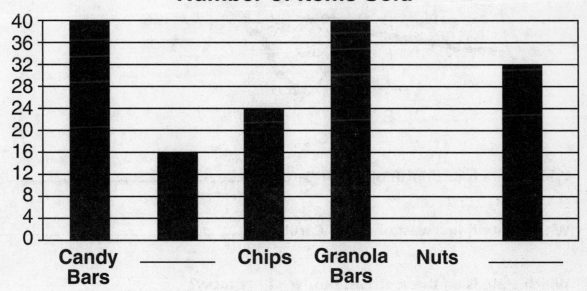

Maps are pictures that tell you where different places are located. The progress chart on page 8–9 is an example of a map that shows the parts of this book.

Directions: Below is a map of part of the eastern United States. Use the map to answer the questions that follow.

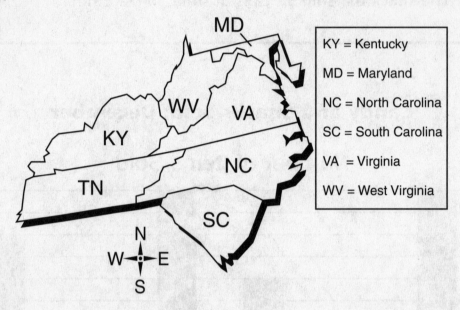

KY = Kentucky

MD = Maryland

NC = North Carolina

SC = South Carolina

VA = Virginia

WV = West Virginia

1.   Which state is just north of North Carolina? _____

2.   Which state is just west of North Carolina? _____

3.   Which state is on the southern border of Kentucky?

_____

4.   What is one state that is on the western border of Virginia?

_____

5.   Which direction would you travel from South Carolina to reach Maryland?

_____

6.   Which direction would you travel from Tennessee to reach North Carolina?

_____

Directions: Below is a map. Fill in the blanks with the information in the box at the bottom of the page.

Wisconsin	North
E	Mississippi River

MAP CHECK 6

Let's pull into a rest stop and check your oil pressure. Now it's time to practice what you've learned.

Directions: Read the weather forecast for five cities below. Then use that information to answer the questions on the next page.

City	Today's Weather	High and Low	Tomorrow's Forecast
Anchorage		high: 64 low: 52	Patchy morning low clouds. Becoming mostly cloudy with scattered showers by late afternoon. South winds increasing to 10 to 20 MPH in the afternoon. High low to mid-60s.
Richmond		high: 88 low: 73	Hot and humid. Slight chance of showers and thunderstorms in the afternoon. High in the low 90s. West wind 5 to 10 MPH. Chance of rain 20%.
Phoenix		high: 100 low: 81	Scattered showers and isolated thunderstorms. Cloudy and cooler. Chance of rain 50%. Highs from the upper 80s to mid-90s. Southeast wind 5 to 15 MPH, becoming southwest 5 to 15 MPH in the afternoon.
Miami		high: 90 low: 75	Hot and humid. Slight chance of showers and thunderstorms in the afternoon. High in the mid-90s. West wind 5 to 10 MPH. Chance of rain 20%.
San Francisco		high: 68 low: 54	Fog and low clouds in the morning. Clearing near the ocean and becoming mostly sunny inland by midday. Highs from around 60 coast side to the upper 70s in the warmest inland areas. Afternoon sea breeze 10 to 25 MPH.

1 The *main* purpose of the chart is to compare —

○ A the amount of rainfall in different cities

○ B the weather in different cities

○ C the humidity in different cities

○ D the number of sunny days in different cities

2 Which question is answered in the column marked "Today's Weather"?

○ F Is it supposed to rain today?

○ G What will the low temperature be?

○ H How strong will the winds be?

○ J What is the capital of Virginia?

3 In the chart, the symbols stand for —

○ A the typical weather

○ B the high temperature

○ C today's weather

○ D tomorrow's forecast

4 Which city is expecting fog in the morning?

○ F Miami

○ G Anchorage

○ H Richmond

○ J San Francisco

5 What would the weather *most likely* be like in Virginia Beach, which is close to Richmond?

○ A Cool and breezy

○ B Sunny

○ C Thunderstorms

○ D Clear and freezing

6 The city in which would you *most likely* want to wear a sweater is —

○ F Richmond

○ G San Francisco

○ H Miami

○ J Anchorage

Directions: Read the passage below and then answer the questions on the next page.

Fruit or Vegetable

1   Fruits and vegetables have been around for millions of years. But did you know that three hundred years ago, the word "vegetable" didn't exist? Back then, any plant that was used for food was called a "fruit." That means in the seventeenth century nobody ever said, "Eat your vegetables, or you're not getting any dessert." Instead, people might have said, "Eat your fruit!" That could be any edible plant, ranging from lettuce to apples, from spinach to oranges, from cauliflower to pears.

2   In the eighteenth century, botanists—people who study plants—examined all of the plants that were called "fruit" and noticed important differences. They realized that some "fruit" came from the ovary of a flower and had seeds. They decided that only these plants should be called "fruit." At the same time, the word "vegetable" was invented. "Vegetables" came to be known as plants that were eaten with meat or during a meal. To sum it up, "fruits" were plants with seeds, and "vegetables" were plants eaten during a meal.

3   Sounds logical, right? Nope. Some vegetables have seeds and are eaten during a meal. For example, cucumbers, eggplants, green peppers, tomatoes, and string beans all have seeds, and you've probably seen them at dinner. So which are they—fruits or vegetables?

4   Good question! In fact, it's a question that the United States Supreme Court had to answer approximately a hundred years ago. In New York City at the time, food importers—merchants who brought food from other countries to sell in the United States—had to pay special taxes to import vegetables, but not fruit. To avoid paying these taxes, one food importer tried to convince government officials that the tomato was technically a fruit and not a vegetable because it had seeds.

5   According to botanists' definitions, this was true. However, according to the Supreme Court it was not. They decided that tomatoes were vegetables because they were generally eaten during the main part of dinner and not for dessert. As a result, the food importer had to pay taxes on shipments of tomatoes.

6   Today, that's how we generally decide whether something is a fruit or a vegetable. Fruits are usually sweet and eaten as a dessert or a snack. Vegetables, on the other hand, aren't very sweet, and we usually eat them during lunch or dinner with soup, meat, pasta, or other vegetables.

7   The next time your parents tell you to eat your vegetables—and you're having cucumbers, pumpkin, squash, beans, peas, eggplant, peppers, tomatoes, avocado, corn, or olives—you could tell them that they should technically be considered fruits. Then again, if you want dessert, you are probably better off just eating them. You don't want your parents to take you to court.

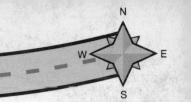

7 Paragraph 5 could answer which question below?

○ **A** How many Supreme Court justices are there?

○ **B** Do tomatoes have seeds?

○ **C** What were the taxes on tomatoes?

○ **D** What did the Supreme Court decide?

8 Paragraph 2 answers which of the following questions?

○ **F** What is the modern definition of vegetables?

○ **G** Where is New York City?

○ **H** What do botanists study?

○ **J** When was the word fruit invented?

9 The main idea of this article is that fruits and vegetables —

○ **A** are difficult to categorize

○ **B** taste good during and after meals

○ **C** are interesting to botanists

○ **D** draw attention from the courts

10 The U.S. Supreme Court became involved in defining fruits and vegetables because —

○ **F** they disagreed with the botanists' definitions

○ **G** it was an interesting legal question

○ **H** a food importer tried to avoid paying taxes on tomatoes

○ **J** people wanted to eat fruit during their meals

11 Check out the map below.

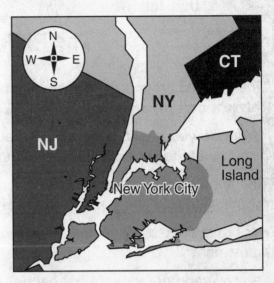

Which state is directly west of New York City?

○ **A** Connecticut

○ **B** New Jersey

○ **C** New York

○ **D** Long Island

12 Look at the chart tracing the different definitions of fruit.

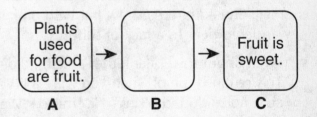

According to the article, which information belongs in Box B?

○ **F** Fruits are used in pies.

○ **G** Fruits are eaten after dinner.

○ **H** Fruits have seeds in them.

○ **J** Fruits are usually eaten with meat.

Directions: Read the passage below, and then answer the questions that follow.

The Polka-Dotted Dress

1   Tina glanced around the busy mall and sighed. "There's nothing I like here, Dad. This just isn't my style."

2   "What do you mean, sweetie?" Her father ruffled her hair. "You have to buy something nice to wear to your mother's wedding."

3   Tina felt a giant lump in her throat. It was the same feeling Tina had had since her mother had told her that she and Mike were getting married.

4   Her father looked concerned. "Are you upset about the wedding? I know it's a big adjustment."

5   She covered her face with her hands. She didn't want to start crying in the middle of the mall. Crowds of shoppers streamed around them. "Can we go somewhere else, please? I'm not going to find anything to wear here."

6   When Tina and her father were back in the car, her dad asked, "Why don't we check out those vintage stores on Fourth Avenue?" Her father knew Tina loved vintage clothing stores. "Maybe they'll have something that's more your style."

7   As they drove, Tina thought about what was bothering her. She wasn't sure if it was that her mom was getting married to Mike, or that Mike's daughter would suddenly become her stepsister. Her parents treated her like she was grown-up, and she liked that. But she also felt very young still. Her father pulled into a parking lot, and they went into the store.

8   Tina loved vintage clothing stores. Racks of old clothing filled the store with a musty smell. She admired a straw hat with pink flowers pinned to its brim, while her father wandered over to a rack of sundresses.

9   "What about this?" her father asked, holding up a red dress with white polka dots. "This reminds me of when you were a little girl and you cried when we wouldn't buy you a polka-dotted bikini." He smiled. "We finally compromised, and you bought a very conservative navy blue one-piece."

10 Tina laughed. "You call that a compromise? You forced me to get that ugly blue swimming suit!" She took the dress from her father and went to try it on. When she came out of the dressing room, she twirled, and the red skirt lifted into a big circle around her.

11 "You look beautiful," her father said, winking at her.

12 Suddenly the tightness in Tina's throat vanished. She wasn't entirely sure why. Maybe it was because her father had remembered the polka-dotted bikini. Even though she was growing up, she knew her parents would always remember her as their little girl.

13 Tina's father suggests that they go to the vintage clothing stores because —

○ **A** Tina is about to cry, and he wants to cheer her up

○ **B** Tina's mother said that it would be her favorite place to shop

○ **C** the mall is too crowded for shopping

○ **D** it is important for her to buy an antique dress

14 The final paragraph of the story answers which question below?

○ **F** How does Tina feel about her mother's wedding?

○ **G** Why might Tina be starting to feel better?

○ **H** How old was Tina when she wanted to buy a bikini?

○ **J** Will Tina share a room with her new stepsister?

15 In the story, Tina tries very hard to —

○ **A** have her father buy her a polka-dotted bikini

○ **B** find a dress her mother will like

○ **C** figure out how she is feeling

○ **D** persuade her father to buy the straw hat

16 Paragraph 7 does *not* answer which question below?

○ **F** Does Mike have a daughter?

○ **G** Where is the vintage store located?

○ **H** Why might Tina be feeling upset?

○ **J** Who was Tina's mother marrying?

17 Which sentence below would fit *best* at the beginning of paragraph 5?

○ **A** Tina's eyes started to well up with tears.

○ **B** Tina's father screamed at her.

○ **C** Tina smiled with pleasure.

○ **D** Tina hoped they would buy the polka dot dress.

18 Why did Tina feel better at the end of the story?

○ **F** Her mother told her the wedding was cancelled.

○ **G** She loved the smell of the clothing in vintage stores.

○ **H** She was allowed to buy the bikini that she wanted.

○ **J** Her father remembered a funny story from her childhood.

MILE 21: LOOKING CLOSELY AT THE TEXT

Directions: Read the passage below. On the next page, use the words listed in the box to decide which part of the passage fulfills each specific purpose.

The History of Money

In the Beginning Was Bartering

Before money was invented, people *bartered.* This means that people traded goods or services they had for goods or services they wanted. Many individuals and organizations still exchange goods and resources, rather than using money.

9000–6000 B.C.: MOO!

Cattle and other animals (like sheep or goats) were the first type of money.

1200 B.C.: Find a Seashell, Pick It Up, and All the Day You'll Have Good Luck!

In China they began using cowrie shells as money, but people all over the world have used cowrie shells as money. Cowrie shells have been used longer and more widely than any other form of currency.

1000 B.C.: Coin Necklaces

China was also the first place that people began using metal coins as a form of money. These coins were made of base metals and often punched with holes so they could be strung together into chains.

640 B.C.: Precious Money

In Lydia (which is now part of Turkey), coins made of precious metals, such as silver, were created. The practice quickly spread to most of Europe.

A.D. 800–900: "You'll Pay through the Nose!"

In Ireland, tax evaders had their noses cut as punishment!

A.D. 806–1535: Potlatch and Wampum

In North America, Native Americans used *potlatch* ceremonies as money. Potlatch ceremonies were rituals in which dances, feasts, and gifts were exchanged. North American Indians also used *wampum,* strings of clamshell beads, as money.

A.D. 1816–1930: The Rise of Gold

As more countries began using paper money, governments made banknotes worth a certain amount of gold so that the paper never became worthless.

currency: money   base metals: metals, like lead and tin, that are not valuable.

Parentheses	Italics
Bold print	Title
Subheadings	Capital letters
Quotation marks	Asterisks

1. How does the author draw your attention to unfamiliar words?

   _____

2. What does the author use to introduce the main idea of the article?

   _____

3. What does the author use to define new words?

   _____

4. What does the author use to break the article into smaller sections?

   _____

5. Where does the author place examples of things?

   _____

   _____

6. What does the author use to note that something has been said?

   _____

7. What does the author use to emphasize different words?

   _____

8. What does the author use to make the titles seem different from the rest of the text?

   _____

MILE 22: MAKING COMPARISONS

You should be able to draw comparisons between two separate passages. To do this, first read each one separately, and then ask yourself what they have in common. A Venn diagram helps you to do this.

Directions: Read the poem and passage over the next two pages. When you're finished, answer the questions on page 110. Then complete the Venn diagram on the final page of the exercise.

One Night at the Pacific

1 Huge waves roll onto the beach,

2 Carrying a deadly lesson to teach.

3 The water breaks hard on the land,

4 Crashing beyond the world of sand.

5 The clouds are mean and scary in the skies,

6 Like looking at a monster in the gleam of its eyes.

7 The night was awful, people ran for cover,

8 Kids sought shelter while the storm did hover.

9 The rain, it seemed to last for ages,

10 Disturbing our homes and rattling our cages.

11 And when we thought the end we'd never see

12 The skies cleared, providing security.

Boating on a Sunny Day

1. When we set sail for the island in the Atlantic Ocean, the sky was as blue as the ink in Father's inkwell. It was perfect weather. The water was calm, and the wind blew steadily from the east, filling our sails nicely. The air was cool, but the sun was out, and soon we were pulling off our sweaters and napping on the front deck of the boat. It was like this for several hours.

2. Father called out the warning. The wind died and then picked up, like someone blowing out birthday candles, a big strong puff. Flat, gray clouds came racing from the west, turning the sky from blue to gray to black. The sun fled. We began to shiver. The sea was frosted with angry whitecaps. Water slapped the side of our boat. It was angry, and our worthy boat rocked back and forth, creaking in pain.

3. We put on sweaters and raincoats. Father put on a wool hat. We put on boots. The wind howled. Before it could push us over, we pulled down the sails. A crow flew out of the darkness, landed on the boat, and began cawing, like a ringing bell, like a warning. Just then, the sea opened its mouth, and we plunged into its salivating jaws. The boat tipped right, then left. Then it spit us out roughly. The boat landed sideways, and water poured into the hull.

4. A strange expression—a mixture of fear and sadness—came over Father's face. He always told us that the sea was unpredictable, but we never believed him. Our sailing trips had always been calm. The ocean sucked us into its mouth again, and this time, we could feel its teeth crunching against the side of the boat. Now we understood why Father had always warned us.

1. What is the theme of "One Night at the Pacific"?

   _____

   _____

2. What is the theme of "Boating on a Sunny Day"?

   _____

   _____

3. How would you describe the mood of "One Night at the Pacific"?

   _____

   _____

4. How would you describe the mood of "Boating on a Sunny Day"?

   _____

   _____

5. Where is personification used in "One Night at the Pacific"? What does it represent in the poem?

   _____

   _____

6. Where is personification used in "Boating on a Sunny Day"? What does it represent in the story?

   _____

   _____

In the left side of the Venn diagram, list three characteristics of "One Night at the Pacific." In the right side of the Venn diagram, list three characteristics of "Boating on a Sunny Day." In the center of the Venn diagram, list three characteristics that are *shared* by both "One Night at the Pacific" *and* "Boating on a Sunny Day."

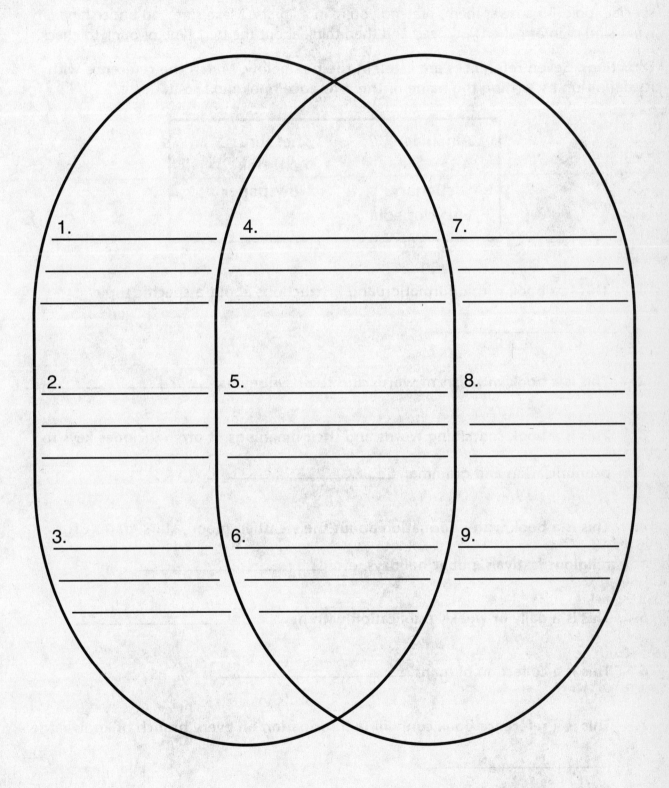

1. _____

2. _____

3. _____

4. _____

5. _____

6. _____

7. _____

8. _____

9. _____

MILE 23: FINDING OUT MORE

On tests in school, you may be asked to decide where to find information about a specific topic. To answer them, pretend you're in a library. Make sure you understand what kind of information you need and then think about the best type of book to check.

Directions: Seven references are listed in the box below. Match the reference with its definition by writing the name of the reference book next to it.

Almanac	Thesaurus
Atlas	Textbook
Dictionary	Newspaper
Encyclopedia	

1. This is a book with information and instructions about a specific topic.

   _____

2. This is a book with lists of words and their synonyms. _____

3. This is a book containing words and their meanings. It often includes keys to

   pronunciation and grammar. _____

4. This is a book with information about the weather, moon, stars, dates of

   religious festivals, public holidays, etc. _____

5. This is a daily or weekly publication with news. _____

6. This is a collection of maps. _____

7. This is a reference book containing information on every branch of knowledge.

   _____

Directions: Read the questions below and fill in the blank spaces with the reference that you would use to answer each question. You may use the terms from the box on the previous page more than once.

8.   What is another word for "amiable"? _____

9.   Where is Libya located? _____

10.   What is the definition of the word "catalyst"? _____

11.   When is the next full moon? _____

12.   How are black holes formed? _____

13.   Who was Frederick Douglass? _____

14.   How is the word "initiation" pronounced? _____

15.   What's happening in the U.S. Congress this week? _____

16.   What are the major events that happened in U.S. history before 1900?

   _____

17.   What's the capital of Greece? _____

18.   What state is south of Georgia? _____

19.   How do you spell the word "cough"? _____

20.   Who was the second president of the United States? _____

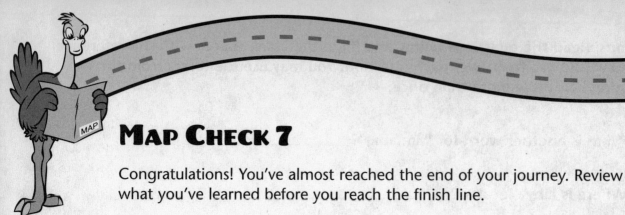

MAP CHECK 7

Congratulations! You've almost reached the end of your journey. Review what you've learned before you reach the finish line.

Directions: Read the following passage, and then answer the questions that follow.

What Do You Remember?

1   Do you ever forget things? Forgetfulness is a common experience. According to recent research, however, inventing things is also one of the mind's tricks. Not only does the mind forget things easily, it also has a tendency to make up things that never happened. This article explores the different tricks that the mind plays with memory.

2   Blocking is what happens when you forget someone's name, or you remember the first letter of a word, but can't remember the rest of the word. It turns out that people have a harder time remembering names than other words. That's because names are random. A woman named Nancy doesn't necessarily look like a "Nancy." The brain stores the sound of the word in a different place from the meaning of the word. If there isn't a strong connection between the two, it can be hard to recall a person's name.

3   Misattribution occurs when the brain accidentally links two different things together, such as a real event and an imagined one. After a tragic plane crash in Amsterdam in the early 1990s, a group of Dutch scientists interviewed their colleagues to see how well they remembered television footage of the crash. Many had very clear pictures of the accident. In fact, there had been no television footage of the plane crash. What the people "remembered" so clearly, they had created in their own minds from reading newspaper articles and talking to friends.

4   People are more likely to remember terrible events than happy occasions. There's a physical reason for this. When you feel stressed out or very upset, your brain builds a stronger connection between the event and the memory. If you think of many unpleasant memories, remember that your brain is better at forgetting the pleasant memories.

5   It's a cliché, but it seems to be true. Happy people have a much easier time remembering happy memories. In contrast, unhappy people often feel that they have been unhappy for a very long time. This is partly because people can't quite remember their past feelings. They assume that their past feelings were similar to what they're feeling in the present.

6   The next time you forget something, don't worry! It happens all the time. The next time you remember something, however, make sure you aren't guilty of making it up!

1 **This article is mostly about how —**

○ **A** it is easy to forget someone's name

○ **B** the brain makes connections

○ **C** the memory can be unreliable

○ **D** terrible events are more memorable than happy ones

2 **People remember unhappy events more clearly than happy ones because —**

○ **F** people don't have many happy events to remember

○ **G** unhappy events are more important than happy events

○ **H** people have a natural tendency to want to have unhappy memories

○ **J** the brain remembers things better in stressful situations

3 **Dutch scientists did an experiment to prove that —**

○ **A** the plane crash was very tragic

○ **B** the television coverage of the crash was effective

○ **C** people can remember things they never saw

○ **D** people should write everything down

4 **"Strong, bad memories" could be another good heading for which paragraph?**

○ **F** 1

○ **G** 2

○ **H** 3

○ **J** 4

5 **According to the article, happy people can remember happy memories more easily because —**

○ **A** they discuss happy memories with their family

○ **B** they mistake their current feelings for past feelings

○ **C** good memories are more memorable

○ **D** they want to forget the bad parts of their memory

6 **If you wanted to read another article like this one, you could check out —**

○ **F** a book about improving your reading skills

○ **G** an essay about terrible tragedies

○ **H** a textbook about the human mind

○ **J** a history of Dutch scientists

Directions: Read the story below, and then answer the questions that follow.

Hector's Ghost

1   Hector was at home alone, and he was supposed to clean his cluttered room before his parents returned from the cinema. Before getting started, however, he decided to explore the attic for a while. For Hector, anything else was more appealing than cleaning his room. He climbed up the creaky ladder.

2   When Hector opened the door to the dim, musty attic, he saw a sight that almost made his blood curdle. It was a pale, white ghost, hovering in front of the window and looking out on the street below. As quick as lightning, he slammed the door and bolted back down the stairs. What was Hector going to do? How could he stay in the house knowing a ghost inhabited it? He paced back and forth with his brow knit in worry.

3   Hector called his friend Ziad Chomsky, who offered to come over immediately and keep him company. Once Ziad arrived, the two boys listened for slightest strange sound. They didn't hear anything. It was terrifying, knowing that your house was haunted, and a frightened Hector collapsed on the couch in exhaustion. Ziad tried to comfort him by suggesting that they call the police since the ghost was technically an intruder.

4   Hector didn't know what to do. If they called the police, he would have to return to the attic. And if they returned to the attic . . . Hector turned pale imagining the ghost again. He didn't want to call the police, but he also didn't want to live with the ghost. Time crawled by, but at last he heard the sound of his parents' car pulling into the driveway. As soon as they walked through the door, he blurted out his story.

5   Hector's parents shook their heads. His mother asked, "Why didn't you just go over to Ziad's house?"

6   "I couldn't leave the ghost in the house alone!" he answered.

7   His father went up to attic immediately. When he returned he announced he had found nothing. The attic was absolutely bare, except for all the junk that they stored up there. Hector had simply mistaken the thin white curtain for a ghost.

8   "Next time, you're going to have to think of a better excuse for not cleaning your room," his mother said, laughing. "Seeing an imaginary ghost is not enough to keep you out of doing your chores!"

7 Why did Hector get scared up in the attic?

  ○ **A** His room was very messy.

  ○ **B** His friend Ziad scared him.

  ○ **C** He heard a noise downstairs.

  ○ **D** He thought he saw a ghost.

8 Paragraph 3 could be *best* introduced by which heading?

  ○ **F** Ziad to the Rescue

  ○ **G** A Supposed Ghost

  ○ **H** The Empty Attic

  ○ **J** Mother's Joke

9 If you wanted to check out another story similar to this one, you might look in —

  ○ **A** a dictionary entry for "ghosts"

  ○ **B** an advice book on cleaning

  ○ **C** a book of amusing short stories

  ○ **D** a collection of true ghost stories

10 The main idea of this story is that Hector —

  ○ **F** wouldn't have gotten scared if he had done his chores

  ○ **G** is glad to see his parents come home

  ○ **H** went to the attic to check out his parents' things

  ○ **J** should have listened to the advice of Ziad

11 Hector didn't call the police because —

  ○ **A** the police don't investigate things like ghosts

  ○ **B** he thought his parents would be upset with him

  ○ **C** he was afraid of having to go to the attic again

  ○ **D** Ziad told him it would be a bad idea

12 "Home Alone" would *probably* be the best heading for which paragraph?

  ○ **F** 1

  ○ **G** 2

  ○ **H** 3

  ○ **J** 4

13 Hector's father goes to the attic —

  ○ **A** to bring down some boxes

  ○ **B** to prove there is no ghost

  ○ **C** to make sure it's clean

  ○ **D** to scare Hector and Ziad

14 Hector went up into the attic because he —

  ○ **F** heard something rattling

  ○ **G** was in search of ghosts

  ○ **H** wanted to put off his chores

  ○ **J** needed to find a broom

Directions: Read the following poem, and then answer the questions that follow.

A London Thoroughfare. 2 A.M.

by Amy Lowell

1 They have watered the street,
2 It shines in the glare of lamps,
3 Cold, white lamps,
4 And lies
5 Like a slow-moving river,
6 Barred with silver and black.
7 Cabs go down it,
8 One,
9 And then another.
10 Between them I hear the shuffling of feet.
11 Tramps doze on the window-ledges,
12 Night-walkers pass along the sidewalks.
13 The city is squalid and sinister,
14 With the silver-barred street in the midst,
15 Slow-moving,
16 A river leading nowhere.

17 Opposite my window,
18 The moon cuts,
19 Clear and round,
20 Through the plum-coloured night.
21 She cannot light the city;
22 It is too bright.
23 It has white lamps,
24 And glitters coldly.

25 I stand in the window and watch the moon.
26 She is thin and lustreless,
27 But I love her.
28 I know the moon,
29 And this is an alien city.

15 The *best* heading for the final stanza of the poem would be —

- ○ **A** The Ugly Streets
- ○ **B** The White Lamps
- ○ **C** The Lovely Moon
- ○ **D** The Window

16 This poem is *mostly* describing how a woman —

- ○ **F** views the city streets at night
- ○ **G** thinks about the glare of the lamps
- ○ **H** feels about the river
- ○ **J** loves the city of London

17 From the poem, you can conclude that the author is *most* at ease with —

- ○ **A** bright lamps
- ○ **B** cabs
- ○ **C** London
- ○ **D** the moon

18 If you wanted to read more about London, you could check out —

- ○ **F** a travel book about Europe
- ○ **G** a biography of the poet
- ○ **H** a collection of stories about rivers
- ○ **J** an English dictionary

19 The moon doesn't stand out in the city because —

- ○ **A** the tramps don't notice the moon
- ○ **B** the night is too dark
- ○ **C** the lamps are too bright
- ○ **D** the weather is overcast

20 The author *probably* loves the moon because —

- ○ **F** it blocks the bright lamps
- ○ **G** she is familiar with it
- ○ **H** it glitters
- ○ **J** London is crowded

PRACTICE
TEST #1

INTRODUCTION TO THE PRACTICE TESTS

You've finished all of the miles in this book. That means you've practiced all of the important fifth-grade reading skills. Way to go!

To check your answers to questions in the miles, turn to page 170.

When you're ready, it's time to take the practice tests. The practice tests in this book are similar to the Virginia SOL Grade 5 Reading/Literature and Research test.

On the actual Virginia SOL Reading/Literature and Research test, you will mark your answers to the questions on a separate answer sheet with a pencil.

HOW TO TAKE THE PRACTICE TESTS

The answer sheet for Practice Test 1 is on the next page. The answer sheet for Practice Test 2 is on page 147. Before you take each practice test, tear out the answer sheet that goes with it. You can cut it out with a pair of scissors if you want to.

Take each practice test as if it were the actual Virginia SOL Reading/Literature and Research test. That means you should not have any books open while taking these tests. Take one whole practice test at a time. If you begin a practice test, don't stop until you are finished with it. Since the Virginia SOL Reading/Literature and Research test is untimed, you can take as much time as you need to finish each practice test. You should not watch television, talk on the phone, or listen to music while you take the tests.

Remember to use the skills that you have learned and practiced in this book. They will help you to do your best. After you have taken each test, have an adult go over it. The answers and explanations to the practice tests begin on page 188. Pay special attention to the explanations of questions that you found hard to answer.

Good luck!

PRACTICE TEST #1 ANSWER SHEET

Completely darken bubbles with a No. 2 pencil. If you make a mistake, be sure to erase mark completely. Erase all stray marks.

1. YOUR NAME: _____
(Print) Last   First   M.I.

SIGNATURE: _____ DATE: _____ / _____ / _____

HOME ADDRESS: _____
(Print)   Number

_____
City   State   Zip Code

PHONE NO.: _____
(Print)

2. YOUR NAME

First 4 letters of last name				FIRST INIT	MID INIT
(A)	(A)	(A)	(A)	(A)	(A)
(B)	(B)	(B)	(B)	(B)	(B)
(C)	(C)	(C)	(C)	(C)	(C)
(D)	(D)	(D)	(D)	(D)	(D)
(E)	(E)	(E)	(E)	(E)	(E)
(F)	(F)	(F)	(F)	(F)	(F)
(G)	(G)	(G)	(G)	(G)	(G)
(H)	(H)	(H)	(H)	(H)	(H)
(I)	(I)	(I)	(I)	(I)	(I)
(J)	(J)	(J)	(J)	(J)	(J)
(K)	(K)	(K)	(K)	(K)	(K)
(L)	(L)	(L)	(L)	(L)	(L)
(M)	(M)	(M)	(M)	(M)	(M)
(N)	(N)	(N)	(N)	(N)	(N)
(O)	(O)	(O)	(O)	(O)	(O)
(P)	(P)	(P)	(P)	(P)	(P)
(Q)	(Q)	(Q)	(Q)	(Q)	(Q)
(R)	(R)	(R)	(R)	(R)	(R)
(S)	(S)	(S)	(S)	(S)	(S)
(T)	(T)	(T)	(T)	(T)	(T)
(U)	(U)	(U)	(U)	(U)	(U)
(V)	(V)	(V)	(V)	(V)	(V)
(W)	(W)	(W)	(W)	(W)	(W)
(X)	(X)	(X)	(X)	(X)	(X)
(Y)	(Y)	(Y)	(Y)	(Y)	(Y)
(Z)	(Z)	(Z)	(Z)	(Z)	(Z)

3. DATE OF BIRTH

Month	Day		Year			
◯ JAN						
◯ FEB						
◯ MAR	(0)	(0)	(0)	(0)	(0)	(0)
◯ APR	(1)	(1)	(1)	(1)	(1)	(1)
◯ MAY	(2)	(2)	(2)	(2)	(2)	(2)
◯ JUN	(3)	(3)	(3)	(3)	(3)	(3)
◯ JUL		(4)	(4)	(4)	(4)	(4)
◯ AUG		(5)	(5)	(5)	(5)	(5)
◯ SEP		(6)	(6)	(6)	(6)	(6)
◯ OCT		(7)	(7)	(7)	(7)	(7)
◯ NOV		(8)	(8)	(8)	(8)	(8)
◯ DEC		(9)	(9)	(9)	(9)	(9)

4. SEX

◯ MALE
◯ FEMALE

© 2002 Princeton Review L.L.C.

The Princeton Review

Practice Test #1

1. (A) (B) (C) (D)
2. (F) (G) (H) (J)
3. (A) (B) (C) (D)
4. (F) (G) (H) (J)
5. (A) (B) (C) (D)
6. (F) (G) (H) (J)
7. (A) (B) (C) (D)
8. (F) (G) (H) (J)
9. (A) (B) (C) (D)
10. (F) (G) (H) (J)
11. (A) (B) (C) (D)
12. (F) (G) (H) (J)
13. (A) (B) (C) (D)

14. (F) (G) (H) (J)
15. (A) (B) (C) (D)
16. (F) (G) (H) (J)
17. (A) (B) (C) (D)
18. (F) (G) (H) (J)
19. (A) (B) (C) (D)
20. (F) (G) (H) (J)
21. (A) (B) (C) (D)
22. (F) (G) (H) (J)
23. (A) (B) (C) (D)
24. (F) (G) (H) (J)
25. (A) (B) (C) (D)
26. (F) (G) (H) (J)

27. (A) (B) (C) (D)
28. (F) (G) (H) (J)
29. (A) (B) (C) (D)
30. (F) (G) (H) (J)
31. (A) (B) (C) (D)
32. (F) (G) (H) (J)
33. (A) (B) (C) (D)
34. (F) (G) (H) (J)
35. (A) (B) (C) (D)
36. (F) (G) (H) (J)
37. (A) (B) (C) (D)
38. (F) (G) (H) (J)
39. (A) (B) (C) (D)

40. (F) (G) (H) (J)
41. (A) (B) (C) (D)
42. (F) (G) (H) (J)
43. (A) (B) (C) (D)
44. (F) (G) (H) (J)
45. (A) (B) (C) (D)
46. (F) (G) (H) (J)
47. (A) (B) (C) (D)
48. (F) (G) (H) (J)
49. (A) (B) (C) (D)
50. (F) (G) (H) (J)
51. (A) (B) (C) (D)
52. (F) (G) (H) (J)

English: Reading/Literature and Research Practice Test #1

The Dance Contest

1 Natasha took a deep breath as she waited in the greenroom behind the stage. Her friend Shelley squeezed her hand and gave her a big smile. Around the room, other girls were silently practicing their routines. It was a big night, the one that they had anticipated for many months. Ms. Chin rushed into the room and told them the show would begin in just five minutes. She wished them all good luck and reminded them they were all winners for working so hard in preparation for the contest. Natasha felt so nervous she could barely breathe.

2 Natasha, who had been hearing-impaired since she was born, had made it to the big dancing contest. Dancing was Natasha's passion. Her parents had signed her up for ballet and modern dance lessons when was just three years old. She had trained herself to feel the vibrations of the music in the soles of her feet. Even though Natasha couldn't hear, she could feel music in her heart.

3 Natasha bent down and touched her toes. Then, she slid into splits, making sure her legs were stretched before she performed. She used sign language to say, "I'm ready!" to her friend Shelley.

4 "You're going to dance beautifully," Shelley signed back to her.

5 "I hope so," Natasha signed. "I don't think I've ever felt so many butterflies in my stomach. I'm so nervous! I can't believe the performance is tonight. I thought it would never come. Now, I'm going to be dancing in front of strangers in less than ten minutes."

6 Shelley gave her a big hug. Natasha closed her eyes and tried to picture her dance routine. She'd chosen her favorite song by Britney Spears. It started slowly but it got faster in the end. Natasha loved the last part of her dance. She got to do three jumps across the stage.

7 She looked around the room. All of the girls looked nervous. They walked back and forth. Natasha remembered her parents' soothing words of advice to her earlier that evening. They told her that if she felt nervous, she should take a deep breath and focus on the feeling of her breathing. After doing this, Natasha felt a lot more relaxed.

8 Ms. Chin tapped Natasha on the shoulder and told her that she was on next. Natasha took a deep breath and walked toward the stage. The lights were very bright, and there were so many people sitting in the audience. Natasha closed her eyes and listened to the music in her heart. Then, she felt the wooden floor start to vibrate. "I'm going to dance like I've never danced before," she told herself.

Go to next page

9 In the audience, Natasha's mother opened and closed her hands above her head. This was her way of showing Natasha that she was clapping. Natasha felt a burst of energy. She stood on her toes and began moving across the stage. The way she moved was like falling leaves. It was slow and beautiful. Then, she felt the music start playing faster. Natasha jumped up and down like a rainstorm. Then, it slowed down again. Natasha slowed down, like someone who was feeling sad.

10 She glanced at her parents. The smiles on their faces were so big that Natasha could see their teeth. She felt so excited. The music quickened, and Natasha danced the last part of the song as hard as she could. She was out of breath, and sweat was dripping off her face. The song she heard in her heart was so joyful. She felt like there was nothing in the world that she couldn't do.

11 Natasha felt the vibrations in the floor beginning to get quiet. She knew it was almost time for her to stop dancing. She did a special movement at the end. She slid down to floor and became very small, like a flower closing its bud after a beautiful sunny day.

12 When she stood up to take her bow, she saw everyone in the audience standing. They had their hands over their head, and they were clapping very quickly. Natasha felt a rush of pride. She had never danced so perfectly before. The audience continued to stand and clap for her. She looked at her parents again. Her mother told her that she was very proud of her in sign language. Tears of joy streamed down Natasha's face as she took another bow.

13 Back in the greenroom, Shelley ran up to Natasha. "I've never seen you dance so well," she signed.

14 "Thank you!" Natasha signed back. She wiped her face off with a towel. "I'm so happy that it's over."

15 When she got into the dressing room, there was a bouquet of roses next to her mirror. The card said, "Congratulations, sweetheart! Your hard work paid off. Love, Mom and Dad." Natasha felt so happy because she had done her best.

Go to next page

1   Paragraph 2 answers which of the following questions?

   A   When did Natasha become hearing-impaired?

   B   How did Natasha hear the music she danced to?

   C   What did Natasha find in the dressing room after she danced?

   D   Why did Natasha feel so nervous in the greenroom?

2   In paragraph 3, the word <u>splits</u> means —

   F   cracks

   G   divides

   H   gymnastics move

   J   ice cream desserts

3   The main idea of this story is how a hearing-impaired girl —

   A   talks with her friend Shelley

   B   does her very best in a dance routine

   C   stretches thoroughly before performing

   D   shares her bouquet of roses with her friends

4   The following statements add intensity to Natasha's feelings about the contest except for which one?

   F   Tears stream down Natasha's face when she is finished.

   G   Natasha has butterflies in her stomach.

   H   There were bright lights any many people in the audience.

   J   Shelley wishes Natasha good luck and hugs her.

Go to next page

5 Natasha began crying after she finished her dance performance because —

A   she felt disappointed in herself

B   her mother signed a special message to her

C   she didn't want to stop dancing

D   another girl said something mean about her

6 Which detail from the story shows that it is set in the present?

F   Natasha had taken ballet and modern dance lessons.

G   The dance performance takes place on stage.

H   Natasha dances to a Britney Spears song.

J   All of the girls are pacing back and forth.

7 Paragraph 7 answers which of the following questions?

A   Why were Natasha's parents clapping?

B   How did Natasha feel during her dance routine?

C   What did Natasha's parents tell her to do to calm her nerves?

D   How did Natasha feel after finishing her dance?

8 The *best* description of Natasha's parents is —

F   overly strict

G   loving and supportive

H   always excited

J   too generous

Go to next page

Beverly Cleary

1   It is difficult to imagine that one of the country's most popular children's book authors was once a terrible reader. Born in 1916, Beverly Cleary moved to Portland, Oregon, in time to start first grade. Beverly read so poorly that she was assigned to the "blackbird" reading group, the lowest one in her first-grade class. Because Beverly's mother was a schoolteacher, Beverly was expected to be a great reader.

2   When it was reading time, Beverly felt her heart racing. She squinted at the words and tried to guess their meaning. She wanted to make her mother happy, but she didn't like reading. The sentences she read ("See kitty. See Mamma. I have a kitty.") put her to sleep. Instead of reading, she worried about how she would be punished for not reading.

3   Beverly's parents tried to encourage her to read. Looking back, Beverly recalls that her mother read to her a lot. "We didn't have television in those days, and many people didn't even have radios. My mother would read aloud to my father and me in the evenings."

4   The school year ended, and Beverly was allowed to continue to second grade but only if her reading skills improved significantly. Luckily, second grade was an improvement. Her teacher was more patient, and Beverly slowly learned to read. However, this author-to-be still found reading boring and never picked up a book outside of school.

5   One dull Sunday when Beverly had nothing to do, she picked up a book called *The Dutch Twins*. She only planned to look at the pictures. What a surprise! The story quickly captured her attention. She wanted to know what was going to happen in the story. She read all afternoon, and after she had finished *The Dutch Twins*, she read another book by the same author.

6   Soon after, the city library became her favorite hangout. She looked for books with stories that were similar to her life. Because she read so much, her teachers began to encourage her. "When Beverly grows up," her seventh-grade teacher pronounced, "she should write children's books." Eventually, her teacher's words of support came true.

7   Since Beverly began writing, she has published more than thirty books that have sold over 10 million copies. Many of her books have won awards, including the Laura Ingalls Wilder Award and the Newberry Medal.

8   Beverly Cleary grew from a little girl who didn't like to read into one of the United States's most beloved authors, whose books encourage children to read.

Go to next page

9 Which of the following headings would fit *best* for the sixth paragraph?

A Successes

B Teacher's Advice

C Turning Point

D Difficulties

10 The "blackbird" reading group was —

F the outdoor reading club

G Beverly's favorite activity

H the lowest reading group

J the highest reading group

11 You could change the word <u>support</u> from paragraph 6 to —

A praise

B work

C aid

D comment

12 The author's purpose in writing this story about Beverly Cleary was *most likely* to —

F describe a difficult child

G review Beverly's books

H relate a terrifying story

J inspire children to read

13 Which of the following sentences would be the *best* one to end the third paragraph?

A Obviously this made it difficult for her to focus on the stories.

B This didn't make a difference because Beverly still hated reading.

C Her story provides all of us with motivation to read and write more.

D These are both the highest awards that a book can receive.

14 You can conclude that Beverly's seventh-grade teacher played an important role in her life from the *fact* that —

F Beverly Cleary's mother had been a teacher

G Beverly's second-grade teacher was patient with her

H she put her in the low reading group

J she encouraged Beverly to become a writer

15 Paragraph 7 answers which question?

A What was the name of the first book that Cleary liked?

B Where did Cleary live when she was young?

C How many copies of Cleary's books have sold?

D How old is Beverly Cleary?

Go to next page

Making Maple Syrup

1   Bundled up in scarf and mittens, Noel follows his mother into the woods. It's still cold enough that Noel can see his breath, and the last remains of snow crunch underneath his feet. Armed with buckets and spouts, Noel and his mother are heading for their maple trees. "I can't wait for the first batch of maple syrup to be done!" Noel tells his mother. She smiles, even though she knows how much hard work lies ahead of them.

2   Maple syrup is made by collecting sap from maple trees. It's an old tradition that dates back to the Native Americans who originally lived in America. Making gashes in trees, Native Americans would drain the sap from maple trees and then add hot stones to help the sap thicken and turn into syrup.

3   Today maple syrup is still time-consuming to make. The sap is the food that the tree made during the summer. Stored in the roots where it turns into sugar, the sap begins to rise up through the tree trunk in the early spring. This is the perfect time to begin collecting the sap.

4   Hard or rock maples produce the highest quality sap for making maple syrup because the sap they produce is sweeter than the sap produced by other types of maple trees. Other factors that affect the quality of the sap are the health, size, and age of the tree. Weather also plays a role. The best time to collect maple sap is when nights are cold and days are 15 to 20°F above freezing.

5   Noel and his mother move from tree to tree, making small holes about three feet from the ground in the trunks of the maple trees. They then put their spouts into the holes so that the sap can flow out of the holes down the spouts. Buckets are hung to collect the sap. Once the buckets are full, Noel and his mother will boil the sap in large pans. In order to make maple syrup, the liquid sap has to reach 219°F. To make maple sugar for candy, it must be boiled much longer.

6   Later that day, Noel checks his buckets. They have barely two inches of sap in them. Noel knows that making maple syrup requires a lot of maple sap. To make one gallon of maple syrup, you need about 35 gallons of sap. This is because most of the sap is water, which evaporates when it is boiled. Each healthy tree produces about 40 gallons of sap each year.

7   When Noel finally gets to sample their maple syrup, <u>dribbled</u> over waffles, pancakes, and even ice cream, he will savor it, knowing just how hard he and his mother had to work to make it.

Go to next page

16 From the description of Noel in the first paragraph, readers will *most likely* —

F understand how to make maple syrup

G realize that the story occurs in the cold

H learn about how to tap a maple tree

J figure out Noel's grade in school

17 Why did the author write paragraphs 2 and 3?

A To describe Noel and his mother

B To explain why Noel and his mother are walking to the woods in the cold

C To encourage readers to put maple syrup on their pancakes and ice cream

D To contrast sap and sugar

18 At the end of the passage, how would you describe Noel?

F Cold but happy

G Excited but patient

H Sad and tired

J Hurried and greedy

19 Which sentence from the passage provides the *best* support for the inference that Noel and his mother are working in the woods in late March?

A Armed with buckets and spouts, Noel and his mother are heading for their maple trees.

B Hard or rock maples produce the highest quality sap for making maple syrup because the sap they produce is sweeter than the sap produced by other types of maple trees.

C It's an old tradition that dates back to the Native Americans who originally lived in America.

D It's still cold enough that Noel can see his breath, and the last remains of snow crunch underneath his feet.

20 Noel and his mother spend the day —

F eating maple syrup on pancakes

G tasting maple syrup from their trees

H preparing their maple trees to give sap

J boiling the sap into sugar

Go to next page

21 This passage is not only interesting but also educational because the author —

A provides recipes in the middle of the passage

B tells a story about a real activity

C encourages people to eat maple syrup

D shows parents and children working together

22 The heading "History of Maple Syrup" would *best* be placed before which paragraph?

F 6

G 5

H 4

J 2

23 Paragraph 6 answers which of the following questions?

A What is the process for making maple syrup?

B When is the best time of year to collect sap from trees?

C About how much sap is needed to make a gallon of syrup?

D What kind of maple trees provides the best sap for syrup?

24 In paragraph 7, what does the word <u>dribbled</u> mean?

F Washed

G Poured

H Mixed

J Bounced

Go to next page

The Great Rift

1   Back in the days when buffalo roamed the plains, a young pioneer girl wandered away from her family's homestead. Henrique was tired of sweeping the dirt floor of her family's cabin and playing with her cornhusk dolls. Adventurous, she decided that she would explore the area north of where she lived, which her parents called the "The Great Rift." Henrique walked for hours, collecting pinecones in her handkerchief.

2   As Henrique walked, she heard her stomach grumbling like the sound of distant thunder. In her excitement to leave, she had forgotten to eat. "How will I continue walking without any food?" she thought. Her stomach grumbled again, and Henrique suddenly felt so weak she had to sit down. She found a spot underneath a large pine tree.

3   As Henrique rested, she heard the distant sound of galloping horses. Suddenly, a gray pony streaked by. It continued, then circled back and stopped in a cloud of dust. Clinging to the mane of the pony was a Native American girl about Henrique's age. She wore white moccasins and leather clothing. Frightened, Henrique tried to hide in the shadows of the tree.

4   "Don't be afraid," the Native American girl said. "I heard the thunder of your stomach and stopped to feed you."

5   "You did?" Henrique asked.

6   "My pony and I hear everything," the Native American girl replied. "We ride the plains listening for the smallest sounds of <u>anguish</u>. Come and ride with me." She patted the pony.

7   Henrique climbed on the back of the pony. The Native American girl cried out in a language that Henrique didn't understand, and the pony began galloping. They traveled for many miles before descending into the canyon. The path to the bottom was steep, but the pony was surefooted. Before night fell, Henrique was sitting next to a stream eating fruits and vegetables from the Native Gardens. Henrique ate for an hour, smiling at her new friend.

8   "People think the canyon is empty," the Native American girl giggled, "which is why we plant our gardens down here. They are safe from thieves."

9   After Henrique finished eating, she felt her eyelids grow heavy and began to sleep. When woke up, she was in bed in her family's cabin. Next to her were the pinecones she had collected, but she could barely remember the Native American girl or the canyon. It all seemed like a dream.

Go to next page

25 Why did the Native American girl stop her pony in paragraph 3?

A She wanted to show Henrique the secret gardens.

B Henrique called to the girl's pony and made it stop.

C Henrique was stealing pinecones that didn't belong to her.

D She could tell that Henrique was in trouble.

26 What is the *most likely* description of how Henrique felt about the Native American girl after they reached the Native Gardens?

F Frightened by the girl and her horse

G Thankful for the food and the girl's help

H Unsure whether the girl and the gardens were real

J Happy with the girl and wanting never to return home

27 Which of the following sentences would fit *best* at the end of paragraph 3?

A Buffalo were wiped out over 100 years ago.

B Many myths seem like dreams.

C She felt very satisfied after the meal.

D She wished she had never left home.

28 To discover where Henrique is going when she leaves her house, you could —

F read the final paragraph very closely

G analyze the conversation with the Native American girl

H skim for the name of a place at the beginning of the story

J skim the description of the journey on the pony

29 The word <u>anguish</u> from paragraph 6 means —

A pain

B life

C happiness

D sadness

Go to next page

30 You could find another story like "The Great Rift" in a —

F dictionary entry about ponies

G reference book on gardens

H history of the western United States

J book of pioneer tall tales

31 The author *probably* wrote this story in order to —

A tell a mysterious story set in a place called the Great Rift

B describe in detail the life of pioneers

C tell the reader how to find the Native Gardens

D tell a scary story about a girl from many years ago

32 Paragraph 1 does not answer which of the following questions?

F Why did Henrique wander away from her cabin?

G What were Henrique's dolls made of?

H Why did Henrique stop walking?

J What did Henrique collect while she walked?

33 Because Henrique forgot to eat, the Native American girl —

A ignored her cries for help

B traded her food for pinecones

C took her on a journey to find food

D showed her the way home

Go to next page

Island Life

You might think I'm lonely

Living on an island in the sea

But here's a little secret

Island life amuses me

1   I live on an island called Obstruction. It is off the coast of Washington. Living on an island is a unique experience. Obstruction is a dry island. That means there are not any lakes or rivers.

2   Behind our house is a well that supplies us with water. The well water is limited, so we also have rain barrels that collect water when it rains. We use this water for bathing, washing things, and watering our garden.

3   My father built our house, which is three stories tall. Because we don't have electricity, we heat our house with a wood-burning stove. One of my jobs is to help my father chop wood. It's hard work, but it gives me a sense of satisfaction to see the wood stacked up high and to know that we have enough fuel for the winter.

4   Luckily, we also have a diesel generator. When we turn on the generator, we can turn on lights, and I can use my computer. We don't have a regular phone though. Unfortunately, there are no phone lines on the island. That means we have to use a cell phone. That's strange, isn't it?

5   The other strange thing is that there is no grocery store on Obstruction. We have to sail our boat to another island to buy food and supplies. As you can imagine, we buy huge quantities of food and supplies. It's no fun to run out of milk or bread when the store is a boat ride away.

6   There are twelve other houses on Obstruction, but we're the only people who live on the island year-round. The other families use their houses during the summer. As you can imagine, summer is my favorite season. Then, there are many other children for me to play with.

7   My friends and I do all sorts of fun things. Sometimes, we explore the island. Because it's small, we can go wherever we want. My friend Jenny and I like to follow the deer paths to the blackberry bushes in the center of the island. In August, when the berries get fat and ripe, we pick buckets of blackberries and make blackberry pie.

Go to next page

8 We also like to dig for clams. To do this, we first read the tide charts to find out when there will be a low tide and more of the beach will be exposed. Then, we head down with our shovels and buckets. The clams are buried in the sand, but they send up little streams of water. We dig in the spots where we see spurts. The best kinds of clams are steamers; they're small and thin, and they have beige-colored shells. Afterwards, we boil them and eat them dipped in butter.

9 Of course, we always have to visit the tide pools at the north end of our beach. Tide pools are left behind when the tide goes out. Water is trapped behind rocks along with all kinds of interesting sea creatures, like starfish, jellyfish, and sea anemones. Once, Jenny and I saw an octopus. That was a scary sight! Its eight arms were covered in suction cups.

10 You're probably wondering whether I go to school. Of course! Except instead of walking or hopping on a school bus, I hop on the school boat. It's a little motorboat that picks up children from all the small islands and takes them to the big one. Once we dock, I ride a school bus. When I get a little older, my parents say I can kayak to school on sunny days.

Go to next page

34 If your teacher wanted you to skim an article, what would you do?

F Read the article backwards.

G Take careful notes on each paragraph.

H Read quickly, noting the main ideas.

J Only read the title and introduction.

35 Reading this article, it is possible to conclude that —

A the narrator and his or her family prefer to use cell phones

B grocery shopping is time-consuming for the family

C steamers are the hardest kind of clams to find

D everyone lives on Obstruction Island year-round

36 Review this sentence from the passage.

> Unfortunately, there are no phone lines on the island.

Which of the following words uses the un in the same way as the un in unfortunately?

F funny

G uncle

H unwise

J under

37 What is the author's purpose in beginning the story with a poem?

A It is what the author's father tells him or her when he or she feels lonely.

B The author is learning to write poetry at school.

C The author and the other island children sing the poem on their boat ride.

D It explains how the author feels about living on an island.

38 The narrator and his or her friend Jenny find clams when —

F their parents tell them to catch food for dinner

G it is low tide and lots of the beach is exposed

H there are no blackberries to pick

J they are learning lessons about the ocean

Go to next page

39 The steps to follow to find clams are shown below.

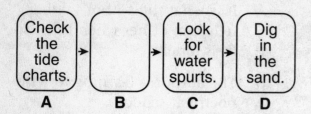

Which sentence below fits *best* in Box B?

A   Check the tide pools.

B   Make clam chowder.

C   Steam the clams.

D   Collect shovels and buckets.

40 Study the following map.

According to the passage, the island where the author lives is located off the coast of one of the labeled states. What is the name of the state that is directly south of this state?

F   Washington

G   Idaho

H   California

J   Oregon

Go to next page

The Door in the Closet

1 Way, way in the back of my closet
2 Behind the boots and clothes
3 Is a small door with a rusty latch
4 And nobody knows where it goes

5 I discovered the door on an angry day
6 When the weather was very unkind
7 The clouds spit hard and hostile rain
8 I was stuck inside, bored out of my mind

9 The tiny door in the closet held <u>fast</u> at first
10 As if it were warning me to stay outside
11 It creaked as I pushed with all of my might
12 The sound made me want to run and hide

13 Suddenly the door opened with a sigh
14 I heard the happy laughing of a brook
15 And smelled fresh chocolate chip cookies
16 I thought I fell into a storybook

17 "Come in, come in," a squeaky voice coaxed
18 "And close the door quick—you're causing a draft!"
19 I paused for a moment, unsure whether to move
20 "Don't be afraid, we don't bite," the voice said and laughed

21 I took a deep breath and squeezed through the door
22 I opened my eyes and looked all around
23 I blinked and could barely believe what I saw
24 Coconut grass and candy trees grew from the ground

25 "Welcome to candy world," peeped a marshmallow chick
26 "Eat all you want, just don't make yourself sick!"
27 There were chocolate bunnies and cherry flowers
28 I thought what I saw must be a trick

29 I picked a taffy peach from a licorice tree
30 And gathered cookies from the sugared ground
31 But then I opened my eyes and was back in bed
32 The door in the closet was nowhere to be found

Go to next page

41 Descriptions such as "angry day" in line 5 and "clouds spit hard and hostile rain" in line 7 make the reader realize the —

A temperature outside

B bad mood of the child

C severity of the weather

D time of year

42 How did the narrator of the poem feel after she squeezing through the door?

F Surprised

G Bored

H Upset

J Anxious

43 The *best* way to describe the narrator of the poem is —

A satisfied

B hungry

C cranky

D curious

44 After reading words in the poem such as "unsure," "paused," "rubbed," and "blinked," the reader has a feeling of —

F doubt

G excitement

H confidence

J sleepiness

45 After reading lines 29 through 32, how will the reader *probably* feel?

A Full and satisfied

B Mystified about the events

C Restless and adventurous

D Disgusted with the child

46 The main idea of this poem is that —

F dreams can seem real

G strangers are friendly

H candy makes you sick

J it should rain more often

Go to next page

47 The way that the word <u>fast</u> is used in line 9, its meaning is —

A alert

B quick

C secure

D open

48 The author's purpose in writing lines 24 through 27 was *most likely* to give the reader —

F instructions for growing coconut grass

G a picture of a magical world

H a catchy rhyme for rainy days

J an understanding of chickens

49 Look at the group of words from the poem.

> the door open<u>ed</u> with a sigh

The word below in which <u>ed</u> has the same meaning as the <u>ed</u> in open<u>ed</u> is —

A <u>e</u>ducate

B danc<u>ed</u>

C d<u>e</u><u>ed</u>

D m<u>e</u>ddle

50 When the poet says, "I thought I fell into a storybook" the reader can infer that —

F the poet is clumsy and falls frequently

G the poet has become an imaginary character

H the poet wonders if the candy world was real

J the poet might have tripped over a book

51 The author's purpose in writing this poem was *probably* to —

A tell an amusing story about his or her imagination

B explain the meaning of dreams

C discourage children from eating too many sweets

D persuade children to explore their closets

52 Why was the door in the closet gone in the end of the poem?

F The poet forgot about it.

G The marshmallow chick locked it.

H The poet moved to a different house.

J The candy world was just a dream.

End

PRACTICE
TEST #2

PRACTICE TEST #2 ANSWER SHEET

Completely darken bubbles with a No. 2 pencil. If you make a mistake, be sure to erase mark completely. Erase all stray marks.

1. YOUR NAME: _____
(Print) Last   First   M.I.

SIGNATURE: _____ DATE: ___/___/___

HOME ADDRESS: _____
(Print) Number

_____
City   State   Zip Code

PHONE NO.: _____
(Print)

2. YOUR NAME

First 4 letters of last name				FIRST INIT	MID INIT
Ⓐ	Ⓐ	Ⓐ	Ⓐ	Ⓐ	Ⓐ
Ⓑ	Ⓑ	Ⓑ	Ⓑ	Ⓑ	Ⓑ
Ⓒ	Ⓒ	Ⓒ	Ⓒ	Ⓒ	Ⓒ
Ⓓ	Ⓓ	Ⓓ	Ⓓ	Ⓓ	Ⓓ
Ⓔ	Ⓔ	Ⓔ	Ⓔ	Ⓔ	Ⓔ
Ⓕ	Ⓕ	Ⓕ	Ⓕ	Ⓕ	Ⓕ
Ⓖ	Ⓖ	Ⓖ	Ⓖ	Ⓖ	Ⓖ
Ⓗ	Ⓗ	Ⓗ	Ⓗ	Ⓗ	Ⓗ
Ⓘ	Ⓘ	Ⓘ	Ⓘ	Ⓘ	Ⓘ
Ⓙ	Ⓙ	Ⓙ	Ⓙ	Ⓙ	Ⓙ
Ⓚ	Ⓚ	Ⓚ	Ⓚ	Ⓚ	Ⓚ
Ⓛ	Ⓛ	Ⓛ	Ⓛ	Ⓛ	Ⓛ
Ⓜ	Ⓜ	Ⓜ	Ⓜ	Ⓜ	Ⓜ
Ⓝ	Ⓝ	Ⓝ	Ⓝ	Ⓝ	Ⓝ
Ⓞ	Ⓞ	Ⓞ	Ⓞ	Ⓞ	Ⓞ
Ⓟ	Ⓟ	Ⓟ	Ⓟ	Ⓟ	Ⓟ
Ⓠ	Ⓠ	Ⓠ	Ⓠ	Ⓠ	Ⓠ
Ⓡ	Ⓡ	Ⓡ	Ⓡ	Ⓡ	Ⓡ
Ⓢ	Ⓢ	Ⓢ	Ⓢ	Ⓢ	Ⓢ
Ⓣ	Ⓣ	Ⓣ	Ⓣ	Ⓣ	Ⓣ
Ⓤ	Ⓤ	Ⓤ	Ⓤ	Ⓤ	Ⓤ
Ⓥ	Ⓥ	Ⓥ	Ⓥ	Ⓥ	Ⓥ
Ⓦ	Ⓦ	Ⓦ	Ⓦ	Ⓦ	Ⓦ
Ⓧ	Ⓧ	Ⓧ	Ⓧ	Ⓧ	Ⓧ
Ⓨ	Ⓨ	Ⓨ	Ⓨ	Ⓨ	Ⓨ
Ⓩ	Ⓩ	Ⓩ	Ⓩ	Ⓩ	Ⓩ

3. DATE OF BIRTH

Month	Day		Year			
JAN						
FEB						
MAR	⓪	⓪	⓪	⓪	⓪	⓪
APR	①	①	①	①	①	①
MAY	②	②	②	②	②	②
JUN	③	③	③	③	③	③
JUL		④	④	④	④	④
AUG		⑤	⑤	⑤	⑤	⑤
SEP		⑥	⑥	⑥	⑥	⑥
OCT		⑦	⑦	⑦	⑦	⑦
NOV		⑧	⑧	⑧	⑧	⑧
DEC		⑨	⑨	⑨	⑨	⑨

4. SEX

○ MALE
○ FEMALE

© 2002 Princeton Review L.L.C.

The Princeton Review

Practice Test #2

1. Ⓐ Ⓑ Ⓒ Ⓓ
2. Ⓕ Ⓖ Ⓗ Ⓙ
3. Ⓐ Ⓑ Ⓒ Ⓓ
4. Ⓕ Ⓖ Ⓗ Ⓙ
5. Ⓐ Ⓑ Ⓒ Ⓓ
6. Ⓕ Ⓖ Ⓗ Ⓙ
7. Ⓐ Ⓑ Ⓒ Ⓓ
8. Ⓕ Ⓖ Ⓗ Ⓙ
9. Ⓐ Ⓑ Ⓒ Ⓓ
10. Ⓕ Ⓖ Ⓗ Ⓙ
11. Ⓐ Ⓑ Ⓒ Ⓓ
12. Ⓕ Ⓖ Ⓗ Ⓙ
13. Ⓐ Ⓑ Ⓒ Ⓓ

14. Ⓕ Ⓖ Ⓗ Ⓙ
15. Ⓐ Ⓑ Ⓒ Ⓓ
16. Ⓕ Ⓖ Ⓗ Ⓙ
17. Ⓐ Ⓑ Ⓒ Ⓓ
18. Ⓕ Ⓖ Ⓗ Ⓙ
19. Ⓐ Ⓑ Ⓒ Ⓓ
20. Ⓕ Ⓖ Ⓗ Ⓙ
21. Ⓐ Ⓑ Ⓒ Ⓓ
22. Ⓕ Ⓖ Ⓗ Ⓙ
23. Ⓐ Ⓑ Ⓒ Ⓓ
24. Ⓕ Ⓖ Ⓗ Ⓙ
25. Ⓐ Ⓑ Ⓒ Ⓓ
26. Ⓕ Ⓖ Ⓗ Ⓙ

27. Ⓐ Ⓑ Ⓒ Ⓓ
28. Ⓕ Ⓖ Ⓗ Ⓙ
29. Ⓐ Ⓑ Ⓒ Ⓓ
30. Ⓕ Ⓖ Ⓗ Ⓙ
31. Ⓐ Ⓑ Ⓒ Ⓓ
32. Ⓕ Ⓖ Ⓗ Ⓙ
33. Ⓐ Ⓑ Ⓒ Ⓓ
34. Ⓕ Ⓖ Ⓗ Ⓙ
35. Ⓐ Ⓑ Ⓒ Ⓓ
36. Ⓕ Ⓖ Ⓗ Ⓙ
37. Ⓐ Ⓑ Ⓒ Ⓓ
38. Ⓕ Ⓖ Ⓗ Ⓙ
39. Ⓐ Ⓑ Ⓒ Ⓓ

40. Ⓕ Ⓖ Ⓗ Ⓙ
41. Ⓐ Ⓑ Ⓒ Ⓓ
42. Ⓕ Ⓖ Ⓗ Ⓙ
43. Ⓐ Ⓑ Ⓒ Ⓓ
44. Ⓕ Ⓖ Ⓗ Ⓙ
45. Ⓐ Ⓑ Ⓒ Ⓓ
46. Ⓕ Ⓖ Ⓗ Ⓙ
47. Ⓐ Ⓑ Ⓒ Ⓓ
48. Ⓕ Ⓖ Ⓗ Ⓙ
49. Ⓐ Ⓑ Ⓒ Ⓓ
50. Ⓕ Ⓖ Ⓗ Ⓙ
51. Ⓐ Ⓑ Ⓒ Ⓓ
52. Ⓕ Ⓖ Ⓗ Ⓙ

ENGLISH: READING/LITERATURE AND RESEARCH PRACTICE TEST #2

Learning an Ancient Game

1. With a look of annoyance on his face, Malcolm stands behind his son, Tyson, who is glued to the television. It's been raining all day, but Malcolm is surprised that Tyson doesn't have anything better to do with his time. "Tyson, how about you and I head to the bowling alley?" Malcolm asks.

2. Tyson looks at his father, puzzled. "You've got to be kidding. No one bowls anymore, Dad."

3. "I beg to differ," his father says, chuckling. "It's no accident that bowling has been played for thousands of years." He gives his son a look, and Tyson reluctantly gets up, knowing that he has no choice but to follow his father. On the way to the bowling alley, Malcolm tells his son more about the game.

4. People discovered bowling pins at ancient burial sites in Egypt, dating back to 5200 B.C. No one is exactly sure how bowling got its name. Some believe that "bowling" is related to the Saxon word *bolla* and the Danish word *bolle*, which both mean "round." Many years ago people bowled using very rough equipment wherever they could find a clearing.

5. The object in bowling is to knock down pins by rolling a heavy ball down a lane. The pins, which are called "tenpins," are 15 inches high and weigh at least 2 pounds 14 ounces. They are arranged in a triangle of 10 pins and stand at the end of a 60-foot-long bowling lane. Bowling balls weigh between 9 and 16 pounds and are always 27 inches in circumference.

6. Once they've reached the bowling alley, Malcolm and Tyson change into bowling shoes. Bowling shoes are different than regular shoes because one of them has a leather sole, which is slick and enables the bowler to slide. The other shoe has a rubber sole, which acts as a brake to help the bowler stop. Bowling shoes also protect the lane from damage caused by normal shoes.

7. Tyson's first turn is a disaster. The ball rolls into the gutter before it even gets halfway to the pins. His father reminds him to watch his aim. On his second try, the ball stays straight and knocks over all ten pins. If all ten pins had toppled on his first try, it would have been a strike. Because it took two attempts to knock all the pins down, it's called a spare. His father congratulates Tyson. Tyson's face lights up. With time, he will become a better bowler.

Go to next page

1 The heading "Proper Footwear" would *best* describe which of the following paragraphs?

A   1

B   4

C   6

D   7

2 What is Malcolm's attitude toward his son at the beginning of the passage?

F   Frustrated and shocked

G   Quiet but proud

H   Surprised and delighted

J   Excited but calm

3 The author manages to make a dull subject more interesting by —

A   giving advice for getting a high score in bowling

B   telling an exciting story about a family

C   explaining a game in terms of a father and son playing it

D   showing the father getting angry at the beginning

4 The word "bowling" *probably* comes from —

F   the last name of the man who invented the game

G   the practice of throwing bowls down the lanes

H   ancient burial sites where pins were discovered

J   Saxon and Danish words that mean "round"

5 What statement does the story tell you that would allow you to infer that people have bowled for more than 7,000 years?

A   Bowling balls weigh between 9 and 16 pounds and are always 27 inches in circumference.

B   People discovered bowling pins at ancient burial sites in Egypt, dating back to 5200 B.C.

C   Because it took two attempts to knock all the pins down, it's called a spare.

D   Many years ago people bowled using very rough equipment wherever they could find a clearing.

Go to next page

6 What was the author's purpose in writing paragraphs 1, 2, and 3?

    F To provide a human perspective on the information

    G To explain why Malcolm enjoys bowling

    H To encourage people to bowl instead of watch TV

    J To offer information on the history of bowling

7 After reading the final paragraph of the story, readers can *probably* conclude that —

    A Tyson will go bowling again

    B Tyson's father will win the game

    C Malcolm and Tyson will buy special bowling shoes

    D Tyson will watch television when he gets home

8 In paragraph 5, the word slick can be *best* defined as —

    F sly

    G fancy

    H smooth

    J fast

9 Paragraph 5 answers which of the following questions?

    A What is a strike in bowling?

    B Why Malcolm is frustrated with Tyson?

    C When was bowling invented?

    D How much do tenpins weigh?

Go to next page

The Desert

1   Lewis darted around the house, chasing his lizard Liza. Liza was a gecko with a beautiful sky blue belly. Lewis had found Liza in the cactus garden in front of his house and begged his grandpa to let him keep the lizard as a pet. Grandpa Henry rocked back and forth in his rocking chair, watching the two of them run around. Grandma Juanita was buying fresh tortillas at the market for their weekly taco feast. Lewis loved tacos almost as much as he loved spending the summer in the desert with his grandparents.

2   Lewis, who would start sixth grade in the fall, lived in a city so it was a special treat for him to spend the summer in the desert. When he stayed with his grandparents, he was allowed to stay up late every night listening to the adventure stories on the radio.

3   Grandpa took a sip of his lemonade and grumbled. "Don't let that lizard run under the refrigerator. You'll never find her again."

4   Lewis grinned and held out his hand. The lizard ran up his arm, and the young dark-haired boy put his pet back in the cage. "See, I've already got her tamed," he said proudly.

5   "You think you've tamed her," Grandpa Henry responded. "But lizards are lizards. There's no telling what they'll do. Just be careful. I don't want you shedding any tears over a lost lizard. You'll call your parents crying, and they'll think we're not feeding you enough."

6   Lewis grinned again. He loved his old grandpa. He had the funniest sense of humor, and he took Lewis on long walks in the desert every morning just as the sun was rising over the hills. Because it was an hour before dinnertime, Lewis asked his grandpa if he could play outside in the cactus garden. The cactus garden was full of all kinds of interesting things. Cholla, saguaro, and barrel cactuses grew there, as well as two lemon trees and a grapefruit tree. It was Lewis's job to water the trees every day. He had to drag the hose to the garden every day.

7   Lewis was also working on a secret project. He was building a rock garden. Every day Lewis would wander behind his grandparents' adobe house and look for beautiful rocks. Then he would bring them back and arrange them in interesting formations. So far, he had built a small wall around his favorite cactus. It wasn't easy work! Some of the rocks were big and heavy. Lewis had had to stop and rest a few times on his walk back to the garden when carrying particularly heavy rocks.

Go to next page

8 Today Lewis headed out to the <u>wash</u>. The wash was the best place to find rocks, especially purple and orange ones. The wash was like a natural path through the desert. When it rained, however, the wash could fill with water. Lewis wandered aimlessly along. Determined to return with treasures, he didn't notice that sky was getting dark. Storm clouds quickly filled the sky. Because he was wearing a hat, Lewis didn't feel the first small raindrops. Suddenly, he heard a loud crack. There was lightning! Now the rain was falling in big juicy drops. It felt like Lewis was taking a shower. His grandpa had warned him that the wash was dangerous when it rained. It could fill with water in a matter of minutes.

9 Lewis quickly turned around and headed back to his grandparents' house. It was slow going because he was carrying a big rock. It probably weighed as much as his dog in the city. The ground was also slippery. Lewis didn't want to leave behind the rock because it would be perfect for his wall. The thunder cracked again. He couldn't believe how dark it was. It was raining even harder now. Water was dripping off the brim of Lewis's hat and into his face.

10 Lewis turned around to make sure the wash hadn't filled with water. But he worried, "What if the water suddenly comes rushing down?" He hurried on, turning to look back every couple of steps. He didn't notice the small boulder in front of him, and he tripped. The rock he was carrying home flew from his hands, and Lewis fell. His hands were scratched up, and his knee started bleeding.

11 "I'd better forget about the rock," he said to himself before he started jogging very carefully. When he got back to his grandparents' house, his grandpa was standing at the screen door. He looked very worried. When he saw Lewis's bloody knee, he said, "The lizard and I were wondering when you were coming home. I hope you weren't up in the wash." Lewis didn't answer. "Well, since it looks like you already took a shower, I'll help you get dried off," his grandpa said. Lewis had a lump in his throat that made it difficult to swallow. He hugged his grandpa.

---

10 **Paragraph 6 might help to answer which question below?**

    F How long did Lewis have to water the cactus garden?

    G Did Lewis take a nap in the garden?

    H How many grapefruit were growing on the trees?

    J What kinds of plants grew in the cactus garden?

11 **As it appears in the eighth paragraph, what does the word <u>wash</u> mean?**

    A Laundry

    B Pool

    C Riverbed

    D Clean clothes

Go to next page

12 What sentence from the story informs you that the passage may be an example of historical fiction?

F   Cholla, saguaro, and barrel cactuses grew there, as well as two lemon trees and a grapefruit tree.

G   When he got back to his grandparents' house, his grandpa was standing at the screen door.

H   When he stayed with his grandparents, he was allowed to stay up late every night listening to the adventure stories on the radio.

J   His grandpa had warned him that the wash was dangerous when it rained.

13 Which of the following descriptions does *not* contribute to the idea that Lewis is scared when he is in the wash?

A   At first, Lewis doesn't feel the raindrops.

B   Lewis remembers his grandpa's warning.

C   Lewis turns around when it begins to rain.

D   Lewis falls and skins his knee.

14 Lewis tripped as he was running because he —

F   was worried about getting swept down the wash

G   tripped on his shoelace

H   was hurrying so his grandpa wouldn't get mad

J   knew it had started raining

15 The story "The Desert" is mostly about how Lewis —

A   plays with his pet lizard named Liza

B   plants a flower garden as a surprise for his family

C   realizes how much he loves his grandparents

D   spends the summer missing his home in the city

16 At the end of the story, the *best* description of Lewis is —

F   very adventurous

G   dry and safe

H   upset but relieved

J   disappointed

17 Which question is answered by paragraph 2?

A   What grade is Lewis in?

B   What is growing in the cactus garden?

C   Where is Grandma Juanita?

D   Why did Lewis go out to the wash?

Go to next page

Roberto Clemente

1 The famous baseball player Roberto Clemente never forgot his family or his Puerto Rican heritage. Born on August 18, 1934, in Puerto Rico, Clemente was the youngest of seven children. His father oversaw a sugarcane plantation, and his mother managed a grocery store.

2 Clemente admired his parents enormously. "When I was a boy," he said, "I realized what lovely persons my mother and father were. I learned the right way to live."

3 Part of the right way to live was working hard. Clemente was nine years old when he decided he wanted a bike. He earned the money by delivering milk. For his work, he received only a penny a day. It took him three years to save up enough money to buy the bicycle, but he didn't give up.

4 Clemente brought the same work ethic to baseball. He spent many hours improving his skills. When he was seventeen, a scout from a professional Puerto Rican baseball team spotted him and asked him to play for their team. His pay was $40 per month, plus a $400 bonus for signing.

5 Clemente soon caught the eye of major league scouts. He signed with the Brooklyn Dodgers in 1954 and played in the minor leagues for a year. The following year, he joined the Pittsburgh Pirates.

6 After five years of perfecting his game and getting used to the major leagues, Clemente exploded on the scene. In 1960 he had a strong batting average. He hit sixteen home runs and brought ninety-four runs in. That year, the Pirates won the pennant and the World Series.

7 Clemente was fast on the diamond, and he had a powerful arm. He could chase down a ball from the outfield, throw it forcefully, and get a man out. He often threw the ball over 400 feet to home plate!

8 As a batter, Clemente was also impressive. He was a "spray hitter," hitting the ball all over the baseball field. He left his mark by becoming the eleventh baseball player to get 3,000 hits. In 1971 he received the World Series's outstanding player award.

9 Clemente didn't allow his success on the field to make him forget his past. He took other Latino baseball players under his wing. When he had time, he offered baseball clinics to children in Puerto Rico, teaching them how to play baseball and be good citizens. When he died tragically in a plane crash in 1972, his family honored his spirit by building a sports complex for Puerto Rican children.

Go to next page

18 As it is used in the seventh paragraph, the word diamond means —

F   cutter

G   field

H   shape

J   gem

19 It can be inferred that Roberto Clemente was a great baseball player from the *fact* that he —

A   was born in Puerto Rico

B   got 3,000 hits in his lifetime

C   worked hard delivering milk when he was young

D   helped children learn to play baseball

20 Which of the following sentences would fit the *best* at the beginning of paragraph 7?

F   Clemente was patient at the beginning of his career.

G   Even after his successes, Clemente remained humble.

H   Clemente wowed fans.

J   Clemente had great respect for his parents.

21 The author's purpose in writing this article was *most likely* to —

A   describe how to be a spray hitter

B   provide a history of baseball

C   make the reader feel sad

D   offer biographical information

22 Which heading *best* describes the fifth paragraph in the passage?

F   Family and Values

G   Community Service

H   American Introduction

J   Career Highlights

23 Paragaph 9 answers which one of the following questions?

A   How many hits to Clemente get?

B   When did Clemente sign with the Dodgers?

C   Who did Clemente play for after the Dodgers?

D   When did Clemente die?

24 Being a spray hitter means —

F   swinging the bat quickly

G   hitting the ball to all parts of the field

H   hitting softly and lightly

J   going to bat when another player is sick

Go to next page

Meng Chiang-nu's Journey

1 During the Chin dynasty in ancient China, the cruel emperor Shih Huang decided that he wanted to build a Great Wall to protect his empire from invasion. He ordered all of his subjects to come from across the land and help build the wall.

2 Wan Hsi-liang was living a happy life in the winter with his wife Meng Chiang-nu when he was called to his duty. Meng Chiang-nu heard nothing from her husband after he left. Winter melted into spring. The flowers bloomed, the trees grew buds, and the clouds were high in the warm blue sky. This cheerfulness deepened Meng Chiang-nu's sadness.

3 When summer turned to autumn, Meng Chiang-nu knew it would grow bitter cold in the north. She made Wan Hsi-liang some clothes lined with layers of padded cotton and resolved to take them to him.

4 Meng Chiang-nu set off north, walking day after day. Finally, she came to the Great Wall, a high stone wall snaking through the mountains. Excited, she immediately began asking people about her husband. No one had heard of him. As Meng Chiang-nu walked, she saw starving people whose bones poked out from their threadbare clothes. Finally she met a man who had known her husband. He told her that Wan Hsi-liang had <u>expired</u> while working to build the wall.

5 Meng Chiang-nu fainted and woke sobbing. She wept for many days. Moved by her grief, the workers began to cry with her. Soon the tears and the wails brought on a raging storm that destroyed two hundred miles of the Great Wall. The people were secretly happy. The emperor heard about the destruction and came to punish the responsible party. When he saw Meng Chiang-nu, however, her beauty overwhelmed him.

6 "Will you marry me?" he asked.

7 "I will," Meng Chiang-nu replied, "if you grant me two wishes."

8 The first wish was that he bury Wan Hsi-liang in a gold coffin. The second was that the emperor attend the funeral.

9 Anxious to marry her, the emperor agreed. The funeral march proceeded down to the edge of a flowing river. There Meng Chiang-nu knelt before her husband's grave. Then, quick as a blink, she flung herself into the river. "I had no intention of marrying you," she cried.

10 The emperor flew into a rage and tried to pull Meng Chiang-nu from the swiftly flowing river. When he got near, however, she turned into a lovely multicolored fish. She slipped away easily and swam downstream, following the river to the ocean, where she lived in a peaceful and free world.

Go to next page

25 In paragraph 4, the definition of the word <u>expired</u> is —

A breathed

B outdated

C died

D laughed

26 Which of the following sentences would be the *best* one to add to the end of paragraph 5?

F The emperor became determined to marry her.

G Many Chinese myths are related to the Great Wall.

H This is what happens in myths and fairy tales.

J The emperor hoped she wouldn't turn into a fish.

27 Why did Meng Chiang-nu begin crying?

A She found out her husband was dead.

B The other workers frightened her.

C The man she met stole her husband's winter clothes.

D She was angered that a wall was being built.

28 The author *probably* wrote this story in order to —

F make you want to visit the Great Wall

G describe the life of an adventurous person

H tell readers the legend of a colorful fish

J explain the history of the Great Wall

Go to next page

29 In exchange for marrying Meng Chiang-nu, what did the emperor have to do?

A   Become a fish

B   Give Meng Chiang-nu a gold bracelet

C   Attend her husband's funeral

D   Promise to tear down the wall

30 Paragraphs 1 and 2 do not answer which question below?

F   Why was Meng Chiang-nu sad?

G   Why had Meng Chiang-nu heard nothing from her husband?

H   Why was the emperor building the Great Wall?

J   What was the name of Meng Chiang-nu's husband?

31 To read a similar story, you could go to the library and check out —

A   a poetry collection about fish

B   the entry on China in an atlas

C   a book about different walls

D   a collection of Chinese myths

32 To find the part where the emperor asks Meng Chiang-nu to marry him, you should —

F   reread the first paragraph of the story several times

G   read about Meng Chiang-nu's search for her husband

H   skim for certain key words such as "marry" and "marriage"

J   carefully study the last paragraph of the story

Go to next page

33 Which statement below describes how Meng Chiang-nu *most likely* felt about the emperor?

A Meng Chiang-nu disliked him greatly for playing a role in her husband's death.

B Meng Chiang-nu appreciated the emperor for creating such an amazing wall.

C Meng Chiang-nu was delighted by the emperor's attention and loved him.

D Meng Chiang-nu was grateful to the emperor for giving her husband a proper burial.

34 From the story, readers can infer that the description "people whose bones poked out from their threadbare clothes" means that —

F the people's clothes didn't fit them

G the people were funny looking

H the people were very thin

J the people had large muscles

35 Read the following graph.

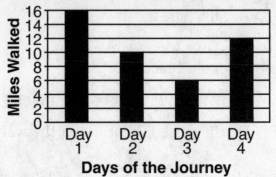

Which of the following statements is supported by the data presented on this graph?

A Meng Chiang-nu walked more miles on the fourth day than on either the first day or the second day.

B Meng Chiang-nu walked fewer miles on the fourth day than on the second or third days.

C Meng Chiang-nu walked as many miles on the first day as on the second and third days combined.

D Meng Chiang-nu walked more miles on the second day than on either the first day or the third day.

Go to next page

Making Money

1 In the cold, damp grass in an old backyard
2 In the muddy, soggy, and brown wet earth
3 Dozens of worms are digging small wormholes
4 They're full of slimy, slithering, wormy mirth

5 No one likes worms; it's a sad and true fact
6 Worms feel slimy, and some worms are fat
7 Worms creep and they can give you the shivers
8 Worms are not friendly like a dog or a cat

9 Now two little boys named Matthew and Scott
10 Are very greedy and like money a lot
11 They dream of jets, mansions, and tons of toys
12 They dream of golden coins filling a pot

13 The little boys come up with crazy schemes
14 To fill their pocket with lots of dough
15 They try to sell their old books and
    broken games
16 They'd sell each other to increase the
    money flow

17 One day they come up with a genius plan
18 They'll pull worms from the ground
    every night
19 They'll harvest worms to sell to fishermen
20 Tasty worms to get the fish to bite

21 So they plop the worms into an old worm barrel
22 And hang up signs, advertising their wares
23 They roll a red wagon to the nearby store
24 The people all shoot them horrible glares

25 These two little boys, they're not very bright
26 When the store doesn't buy their creepy, squirmy goods
27 They close up the worm shop, losing all their heart
28 They head to find spiders and run in the woods

29 Those poor little worms in the old worm barrel
30 They've been shut out to sleep in a cold and dark bed
31 Nobody likes clammy, slimy crawlers
32 But with no yucky worm food they'll all soon be dead

Go to next page

36 Look at this description from the poem.

> filling a pot

Which of the following words uses <u>ing</u> with the same meaning as in the example?

F   <u>ing</u>rown

G   laugh<u>ing</u>

H   r<u>ing</u>ers

J   sw<u>ing</u>

37 The author's purpose in writing lines 9 through 12 was *most likely* to make the reader —

A   come up with ideas for making lots of money

B   feel sorry for worms and other mistreated animals

C   develop a good understanding of the characters

D   learn how Matthew and Scott plan to get rich

38 In the first stanza, descriptions such as "slimy," "slithering," "muddy," and "soggy" give readers a feeling of the —

F   creativity of the boys

G   size of the shed

H   unpleasantness of worms

J   time of year

39 How do Matthew and Scott feel when they can't sell their worms?

A   Hopeful

B   Angry

C   Energetic

D   Discouraged

40 The *best* description of the two boys in the poem is —

F   innocent

G   considerate

H   thoughtless

J   intelligent

Go to next page

41 In the last four lines, descriptive words such as "poor," "dark," "cold," and "dead" create a feeling of —

A   fright

B   optimism

C   happiness

D   anger

42 After reading lines 13 through 16, the reader will *probably* feel —

F   envious about their plans

G   angry and confused

H   amused by the boys

J   tired and bored

43 After reading this poem, you can draw the conclusion that —

A   worms are important to the well-being of the earth

B   greedy boys will be good businessmen someday

C   parents should give their children a lot of money

D   even creepy things should be treated with respect

44 To keep the same meaning, you could replace the word dough in line 14 of the poem with the word —

F   paste

G   batter

H   money

J   pulp

Go to next page

The Muffin Maker

At our bakery, we make up funny songs:

A cherry crisp, an apple pie
A dozen muffins, a marble rye
Chocolate cookies, honey cake
From dawn to dusk, we bake, bake, bake.

1   We make lots of other desserts as well.

2   I mainly help out at the bakery before and after school. During the summer vacation I work there full-time. I'm the official muffin maker. My muffins are out of this world.

3   Our bakery is in Philadelphia, Pennsylvania. My grandpa left Germany before World War II and emigrated here. He came by steamship. In his trunk he carried his prized possessions: his bread pans and marble rolling pins.

4   My grandpa died before I was born, but he left behind Henry's Bakery. (That was his name.) When he first opened Henry's, the bakery specialized in making and selling the kind of dark, thick bread that is a staple in Germany and eastern Europe. This kind of bread is called by funny names, like rye and pumpernickel. My mom says Grandpa Henry was always covered in flour from head to toe. It sounds like he looked like a ghost.

5   My grandma Jenny started making desserts. She was famous for her sweet tooth. One day she told Grandpa that she was hungry for a thick slice of Black Forest cake. Grandpa told her to make some, and from then on, the bakery also became famous for its desserts.

6   My mom and dad took over the bakery when Grandpa got too weak to carry the trays of bread loaves to the oven. I was almost born in the bakery. My mother didn't want to leave for the hospital until she'd taken out a batch of almond cookies. One of the first words I said was yum-yum, which referred to anything that was sweet.

7   It's not too surprising that I'm the muffin maker. My parents called me their little lemon muffin when I was a baby because I was born with bright yellow hair. Making muffins is easy. First, I grease the tins, which means I have to rub butter in them. I use lots of butter so the muffins won't stick. It also makes them more delicious.

8   Then I start working on the batter. I follow lots of different recipes, but some ingredients are the same in all of them: butter, eggs, flour, sugar, and baking soda. I mix the dry ingredients together in one bowl. In another bowl, I mix the wet ones.

Go to next page

9 In some recipes, I have to combine the butter and flour. This is my least favorite part because I have to cut the butter into tiny pieces with a dull knife. Slowly, the butter turns into crumbly little pieces coated with flour.

10 Finally, I slowly add the flour and other dry ingredients to the wet ingredients and stir. I have to stir so much that my hand sometimes hurts. The last step is to spoon the muffin dough into the tins and then pop them into the oven.

11 My parents use giant electric mixers when they bake. Some of the bowls are so big I can hide in them. They make twenty loaves of bread or five cakes at the same time. Since I'm still in elementary school, I have to mix everything by hand. That's okay with me because I think it makes my muffins more special.

12 As the muffins bake, the kitchen smells warm and wonderful. I start on another batch or I work on my homework. When the timer rings, I take the muffins out of the oven and allow them to cool.

Go to next page

45 After reading this article, you can infer that —

A Grandpa Henry owned a bakery in Germany

B Grandma Jenny started the tradition of selling desserts

C Henry's Bakery is haunted by a ghost

D Henry's Bakery only sells different kinds of bread

46 To skim this article, you would read —

F the first sentence in every paragraph

G the title and every other paragraph

H slowly, writing down every word in your notebook

J quickly, noting the main ideas in the story

47 Look at this map.

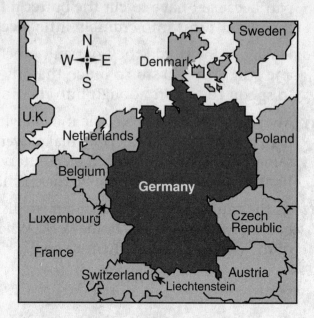

Which country is directly north of where the muffin maker's grandfather came from?

A Czech Republic

B Denmark

C Austria

D Poland

48 Look at the sentence below from the article.

> The butter turn into crumb<u>ly</u> little pieces coated with flour.

Which of the following words uses the <u>ly</u> in the same meaning as in the example?

F <u>ly</u>ing

G nice<u>ly</u>

H fol<u>ly</u>

J <u>ly</u>ric

Go to next page

49 The narrator was almost born in the bakery because —

  A the narrator's mother wanted to finish baking some cookies

  B the narrator enjoys working in the bakery so much

  C the narrator needed to grease the muffin tins for muffins

  D the narrator's family could not afford to go to a hospital

50 This chart shows how to make muffins.

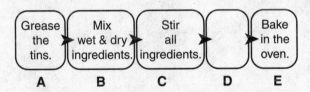

  A Grease the tins. → **B** Mix wet & dry ingredients. → **C** Stir all ingredients. → **D** → **E** Bake in the oven.

  What sentence belongs in the blank Circle D?

  F Add the almonds to the cookies.

  G Allow the muffins to cool.

  H Cut the butter into the flour.

  J Fill the muffin tins with batter.

51 What was the author's purpose in beginning the article with a poem?

  A It reveals the activities and products at the busy bakery.

  B Bakers sing to their bread because it helps it rise.

  C It is the song that Grandpa Henry sang as he baked.

  D This was the first poem that the author ever memorized.

52 The author's purpose in writing this piece was *probably* to —

  F relate a sad story about a child and his or her grandfather

  G invite people to sample the muffins in his or her bakery

  H give a terrific recipe for making muffins

  J describe his or her family and their bakery business

End

ANSWER KEY TO MILES

A   Stories about animals

B   Information on the bus schedule

C   Information about the volcanic eruption

D   Information about skits to do at birthday parties

E   Information about scientific discoveries

F   Poems about animals

G   Information on Florida

H   Stories about young people who play chess

I   Stories about Eliza

J   Information about treasures from the ocean

K   Nursery rhymes

L   Instructions for craft projects

---

1   Nonfiction

2   Fiction

3   Fiction

4   Fiction

5   Nonfiction

6   Fiction

7   Nonfiction

8   Fiction

9   Nonfiction

10 Fiction

Any true (nonfiction) statement about animals would be correct for 11. Below are two examples.

11 Whales are the biggest mammals in the world.

Pandas are an endangered species.

Any made-up (fiction) statement about animals would be correct for 12. Two examples follow.

12 Indian elephants prefer to drink tea.

Kathy the kangaroo only wanted to move to America.

13 Champions of Women's Rights

14 nonfiction

15 Frontier Diary

16 historical fiction

17 Across the Ocean

18 historical fiction

19 The American Revolution

20 nonfiction

21 Abraham Lincoln's Beard

22 nonfiction

MILE 2: WHY DO PEOPLE READ?

To have fun	To gain knowledge	To learn how to do things
Fairy Tales	Autobiographies	Recipes
Plays	Biographies	Art Projects
Poems	Maps	Science Experiments
Myths	Newspaper Articles	Directions
Humorous Stories	Magazine Articles	
	Encyclopedia Articles	
	Schedules	
	Scientific Illustrations	
	Weather Reports	
	Dictionary Definitions	
	History Textbook	

1   a history book

2   A person might read this selection to find out more information about Ghandi.

3   a schedule

4   A person might read this selection to find out when the bus leaves.

5   an encyclopedia article

6   A person might read this selection to learn more about Canada.

7   a poem

8   A person might read this selection to have fun reading a poem.

9   a story

10   A person might read this selection to have fun reading a scary story.

MILE 3: FINDING THE MAIN IDEA

1 Dom missed having waffles for breakfast because he slept too late.

2 Oceans are saltier than rivers for several reasons.

3 Juanita received a big surprise on her birthday.

4 The Big Surprise

5 There are many different causes and symptoms of dehydration.

6 Dehydration

7 Frederick Douglass had a difficult life. He was born a slave, and he worked hard to win his freedom. After he was free, he tried to help other slaves win their freedom.

8 The famous author and champion of the rights of African Americans and women traveled a long way from his humble beginnings.

MILE 4: FINDING SUPPORTING IDEAS

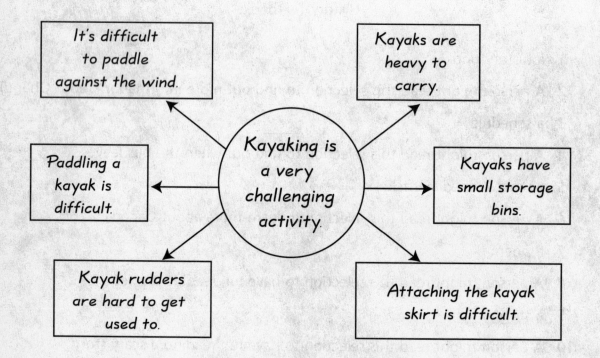

MILE 5: ANSWERING MULTIPLE-CHOICE QUESTIONS

1 B

2 H

MAP CHECK 1

1	B	10	G
2	J	11	D
3	D	12	F
4	H	13	C
5	A	14	J
6	J	15	B
7	B	16	G
8	J	17	A
9	C	18	J

MILE 6: ANSWERING QUESTIONS ABOUT DETAILS

1 Eunice opened the card from her mother because she was feeling bad and thought reading the card from her mother would help her feel better.

2 Rubber is important because it's used to make many different things.

3 Dmitri got frustrated when he was learning to play the guitar because he had trouble reaching and pressing the right strings.

4 Valleys, bogs, riverbeds, and streambeds are the most likely places to find quicksand.

5 One of the causes of side stitches is muscle spasms.

6 You can tell if you're breathing deeply by lying on the floor and feeling your stomach.

7 Some people pretend they're blowing out candles while they run to make sure they're taking deep breaths.

8 Shallow breathing causes side stitches because your diaphragm doesn't expand completely, and your liver is always pulling against it.

9 Lie on the floor and put your hand on your stomach. Take a deep breath of air. If your hand moves up slightly, then you are breathing deeply. If your hand doesn't move, you are not filling your lungs with enough air.

MILE 7: LEARNING VOCABULARY IN CONTEXT

The following words should be matched:

mannerisms ———→ habits

identical ———→ exactly alike

genetic material ———→ chemical molecules

heredity ———→ inherited qualities

environmental ———→ circumstantial

traits ———→ characteristics

MILE 8: PREFIXES AND SUFFIXES

1   preschool

2   disappeared

3   unhappy

4   reread

5   readjust

6   restart

7   disliked

8   return

9   preheat

---

1   badly

2   firmly

3   careless

4   hopeless

5   filthy

6   magically

7   believable

8   loudly

Map Check 2

1	C	10	J
2	F	11	B
3	D	12	F
4	F	13	B
5	C	14	G
6	G	15	B
7	C	16	H
8	G	17	A
9	D	18	H

Mile 9: Making Predictions

1   I think Cassius and Abel are going to get even with Ugali by not choosing him first in kickball.

2   I think Ugali is going to learn his lesson.

3   Do Cassius and Abel follow through with their plans?

4   What happens to Ugali?

5   Ugali doesn't get chosen first for the kickball team. Instead of becoming a nicer person, he begins playing tetherball all by himself.

6   I was surprised by the actual ending. I had no idea that Ugali would start playing tetherball. I was also surprised that he becomes so unpopular by the end of the story.

7   Cassius and Abel do stick to their plans, and they don't choose Ugali.

8   Ugali gets really upset when he isn't chosen for kickball and runs off to play tetherball.

Mile 10: Drawing Conclusions

There are no right or wrong answers for this activity. You could have written anything that is shown in the picture. Below are six examples, even though you only needed four.

1 It's a hot day, and the players are trying to stay cool.

2 Some kids are playing a baseball game.

3 The girl with the braids hit the ball to the outfield.

4 Instead of retrieving the ball, the outfielder is petting a cat.

5 The coach is very angry.

6 The coach is angry at the outfielder who is not paying attention.

---

1 The woman is a cowgirl. She's going to ride her horse at the county fair.

2 The little boy just lost his balloon. He is very upset.

3 The woman is dressed up. She's bringing a pie for the food competition.

4 The man is an entertainer. He eats fire.

5 The man is a farmer. He is bringing chickens to the fair.

6 The woman is a chef. She is going to sell scones at the fair.

7 The man is a businessperson. He is feeling hot and annoyed.

8 The kids are happy to be buying tickets to the fair. They have many coins.

---

1 She feels very scared and nervous.

2 She is afraid of the pig because it seems gross and dangerous.

3 Tali would feel disgusted if the pig rolled over on her. She would probably throw up.

4 Tali is singing the song in hopes of drawing someone's attention and getting help to escape from the pig.

5 She doesn't want to wake up the pig.

MILE 11: DRAWING CONCLUSIONS ABOUT AUTHORS' CHOICES

1 The author has made this story enjoyable to read by providing details about how Basil feels about the ocean and the forest. It is also enjoyable because it is exciting. The ocean is unpredictable, and Barnaby and Basil have to leave.

2 The details show how much Basil loves the ocean. They also show why she will miss it.

3 They tell us that Basil is very tired and unhappy.

4 The last line shows us that Basil is finally happy enough to sleep.

5 The author's purpose in writing this selection was to entertain the reader.

6 It stresses the fact that someone is very sleepy.

7 The author's purpose in writing this selection was to provide information and be persuasive.

8 It provides a detail to support the idea that people should wear their seatbelts.

9 The author's purpose in writing this selection was to entertain the reader.

10 It's funny, and it helps show that the story is supposed to be funny.

11 The author's purpose in writing this selection was to relate a personal experience.

12 It shows that hiking was difficult for the narrator.

13 The author's purpose in writing this selection was to provide information.

14 It provides more information about kaleidoscopes.

MAP CHECK 3

1	B	10	F
2	G	11	C
3	C	12	G
4	G	13	D
5	D	14	J
6	J	15	A
7	C	16	G
8	H	17	D
9	D	18	F

Mile 12: Plot, Setting, Characters, and Theme

1   Character: Description:
    Juan   Hardworking
    Tela   Nice

2   The story takes place in a barn at the county fair.

3   The story takes place in modern times.

4   The main conflict is that Juan is afraid that Henrietta will do something bad during the competition.

5   When Juan is talking to Tela, he realizes that Henrietta is well trained and won't do anything wrong.

6   Juan knows that he's worked so hard that Henrietta will do well in the competition.

Mile 13: Getting Inside a Character's Head

1   He feels that she is beautiful.

2   "Charaxos was hypnotized by her beauty."

3   He feels angry.

4   "Charaxos tightened his fists when he heard how she had been mistreated."

5   He feels happy for Rhodopis, but also sad because he is going to lose her.

6   "Charaxos, for his part, paced back and forth in the garden with a smile pasted on his face. His stomach churned, and his heart seemed to be shriveling. But when Rhodopis swept out of the house, looking more radiant than ever, Charaxos swallowed the lump in his throat and embraced her . . ."

Generous	Angry	Sad
He buys her lots of things such as jewels and clothing.	"Charaxos tightened his fists when he heard how she had been mistreated."	His heart feels like it is shriveling.
He builds her a house.		He has a lump in his throat.
He plants a garden for her.		He says good-bye with tears.
He worked so that he could shower gifts on her.		

Map Check 4

1	C	7	A	13	A
2	F	8	H	14	F
3	C	9	B	15	D
4	G	10	F	16	F
5	D	11	C	17	C
6	J	12	H	18	J

Mile 14: Metaphor, Simile, and Personification

1 **Simile**: a comparison between two different things that is formed with "like," "as" or "than."

2 **Metaphor**: a comparison between two things that is usually formed with a "to be" verb.

3 **Personification**: a figure of speech that gives animals, ideas, or objects human qualities and characteristics.

1 Simile

2 Personification

3 Metaphor

4 Personification

5 Simile

6 Personification

7 Metaphor

8 Metaphor

9 Simile

10 Personification

11 Simile

12 The underlined selection shows that the mother got very mad.

13 Personification

14 The underlined selection shows that the house seemed sad because the Jins were leaving.

15 Metaphor

16 The underlined selection shows that the photographer is asking his model to shine brightly for the camera.

17 Simile

18 The underlined selection shows that the seagulls were making a lot of noise.

19 Metaphor

20 The underlined selection shows that the day is a nice surprise for Edu.

21 Personification

22 The underlined selection shows that the moon was smiling down at the hikers, meaning they were having a pleasant walk.

MILE 15: MOOD

1 Mysterious

2 Simile: "The old woman cackled like a hen . . ."

3 Humorous or nonsensical

4 Metaphor: "Eliza Elizabeth was an elegant dandelion."

5 Serious

6 Simile: "The principal's face darkened suddenly like a storm sweeping across a sky."

7 Nonsensical

8 Simile: "Don't be as sharp as a butter knife."

9 Sorrowful

10 Personification: "he wanted to go home" or "cast his sad eyes down toward the ground."

MILE 16: ELEMENTS OF POETRY

1 Rhyme

2 Mood

3 Stanza

4 Rhythm

5 Theme

6 2

7 4

8 2 and 3

9 happy

10 Weather can't keep the author from feeling happy.

MAP CHECK 5

1	D	10	G
2	G	11	A
3	B	12	F
4	J	13	D
5	B	14	J
6	H	15	B
7	D	16	J
8	F	17	B
9	C	18	J

MILE 17: USING CHARTS WITH STORIES

1   *An American Dictionary of the English Language*

2   Standardized spelling for many words

3   more than 100 million

4   Contained standard ways to pronounce words

MILE 18: USING CHARTS WITH FACTS

1   903

2   Chicago

3   8 A.M.

4   4:10 P.M.

5   Boston

Bollen Valley: At the midway point is a one-room schoolhouse that was used in the nineteenth century.

Cat's Meow: 6.5 miles

Ann's Peak

Three Streams: ●

MILE 19: READING GRAPHS

1 PE

2 Social Studies

3 Math and Science

4 25%

5 More students like the other classes combined.

6 You can tell by looking at the size of the slices on the pie graph.

Candy and Snacks Sold: December

Number of Items Sold

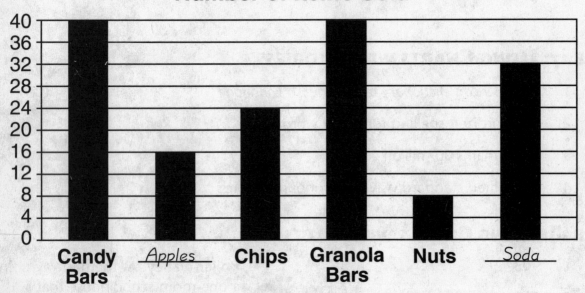

MILE 20: READING MAPS

1 Virginia

2 Tennessee

3 Tennessee

4 Kentucky or West Virginia

5 North

6 East

MAP CHECK 6

1 B

2 F

3 C

4 J

5 C

6 J

7 D

8 H

9 A

10 H

11 B

12 H

13 A

14 G

15 C

16 G

17 A

18 J

MILE 21: LOOKING CLOSELY AT THE TEXT

1 italics

2 title

3 asterisks

4 subheadings

5 parentheses

6 quotation marks

7 capital letters

8 bold print

MILE 22: MAKING COMPARISONS

1   The ocean can be very dangerous, but then the weather can change.

2   The weather can change quickly, turning a beautiful day into a stormy one.

3   Frightening

4   Chaotic

5   Personification is used when the author describes the clouds as "mean and scary in the skies / Like looking at a monster in the gleam of its eyes." It represents the clouds.

6   Personification is used when the author says that "the sea opened its mouth, and we plunged into its salivating jaws. Then it spit us roughly out." This makes the sea seem like it is trying to devour the boat.

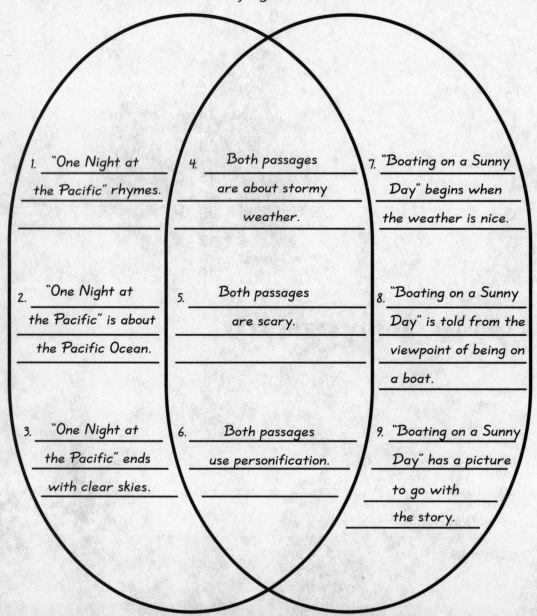

1. "One Night at the Pacific" rhymes.

2. "One Night at the Pacific" is about the Pacific Ocean.

3. "One Night at the Pacific" ends with clear skies.

4. Both passages are about stormy weather.

5. Both passages are scary.

6. Both passages use personification.

7. "Boating on a Sunny Day" begins when the weather is nice.

8. "Boating on a Sunny Day" is told from the viewpoint of being on a boat.

9. "Boating on a Sunny Day" has a picture to go with the story.

MILE 23: FINDING OUT MORE

1	Textbook	11	Almanac
2	Thesaurus	12	Encyclopedia
3	Dictionary	13	Encyclopedia
4	Almanac	14	Dictionary
5	Newspaper	15	Newspaper
6	Atlas	16	Textbook
7	Encyclopedia	17	Atlas
8	Thesaurus	18	Atlas
9	Atlas	19	Dictionary
10	Dictionary	20	Textbook

MAP CHECK 7

1	C	11	C
2	J	12	F
3	C	13	B
4	J	14	H
5	B	15	C
6	H	16	F
7	D	17	D
8	F	18	F
9	C	19	C
10	F	20	G

PRACTICE TEST #1
ANSWERS AND
EXPLANATIONS

THE DANCE CONTEST

1   **A**   This question asks you to look at the second paragraph. The second paragraph says that Natasha has been hearing-impaired since she was born. Consider which of the questions stated in the answer choices this information answers. Get rid of **B** because how Natasha hears music isn't answered by the information in this paragraph. Cross off **C** because what Natasha finds in the dressing room isn't answered by the information in this paragraph. Get rid of **D** because why Natasha feels nervous isn't answered by the information in this paragraph. The correct answer choice is **A**.

2   **H**   This question asks you to identify the meaning of the word "splits." Find the word "splits" in the third paragraph. Replace the word "splits" with each of the answer choices. Get rid of **F** because Natasha doesn't slide into cracks. Cross off **G** because Natasha can't slide into divides. Eliminate **J** because Natasha doesn't slide into ice cream desserts. The correct answer choice is **H** because Natasha does slide into a gymnastics move.

3   **B**   Consider the main idea of the story. Get rid of **A** and **C** because they are both details and only describe a part of the story. Cross off **D** because Natasha doesn't share her flowers. Therefore, the correct answer choice is **B**.

4   **J**   Remember to read each question carefully. This question uses the word "except." That means you should get rid of all the answer choices that add intensity to Natasha's feelings about the contest and choose the answer choice that does not add intensity to Natasha's feelings about the contest. Get rid of **F**, **G**, and **H** because these answer choices add intensity. Answer choice **J** is correct because it does not add intensity.

5   **B**   Return to the story and locate where Natasha begins to cry. According to the story, tears stream down Natasha's face right after her mother signs that she was very proud of Natasha. Get rid of **A**, **C**, and **D** because they are not supported by the information in the story.

6   **H**   Carefully consider each answer choice. Get rid of **F**, **G**, and **J** because these answer choices do not show that the story is set in the present. These answer choices could refer to a story taking place during many different time periods. Answer choice **H** is correct because Britney Spears is a modern, present-day performer. Therefore, answer choice **H** shows that the story is set in the present.

7 C This question asks you about the seventh paragraph. The seventh paragraph mentions that Natasha's parents told her to breathe deeply and focus on her breathing when she is nervous. Consider which of the questions stated in the answer choices this information answers. Get rid of **A**; why Natasha's parents were clapping isn't answered by the information in this paragraph. Cross off **B** because the paragraph doesn't tell you how Natasha felt during her dance routine. Get rid of **D** also because how Natasha felt after dancing isn't answered by the paragraph. The correct answer choice is **C**.

8 G Consider the actions of Natasha's parents in the story. Natasha's parents clap for her, sign her special messages, and give her flowers. Get rid of **F**, **H**, and **J** because they are not overly strict, always excited, or too generous. The correct answer choice is **G**.

BEVERLY CLEARY

9 C The sixth paragraph describes the day that Cleary realized she liked to read. Before the sixth paragraph, you learn about Cleary's difficulties. And after the sixth paragraph, you learn about her successes and her teacher's advice. That means the correct answer choice is **C**, *Turning Point.*

10 H Skim the story for the key word "blackbird." This key word first appears in the first paragraph. If you read carefully, you'll see that the story says that Cleary was in the lowest reading group. That makes answer choice **H** correct.

11 A Find the word "support" in the sixth paragraph. Then replace the word "support" with each of the answer choices. Get rid of **B** because "words of work" does not make sense. Cross off **C** because "words of aid" does not make sense. Get rid of **D** because "words of comment" also does not make sense. Answer choice **A** is correct because "words of praise" makes the most sense.

12 J This question asks about the author's purpose. Get rid of **F** because the passage does not describe a difficult child. The passage describes difficulties with reading that Beverly had as a child. Cross off **G** because the passage does not review Beverly's books. Get rid of **H** too, because the passage does not tell a terrifying story. The correct answer choice is **J** because the passage *does* inspire children to read.

13 B The third paragraph is about the efforts of Beverly's mother to encourage Beverly to read. Despite these efforts, Beverly still doesn't like to read. Get rid of **A**, **C**, and **D** because they are ideas that are talked about in other paragraphs. The correct answer choice is **B**.

14 J Beverly's seventh-grade teacher encouraged her to become a writer, and Beverly did. That means that Beverly's seventh-grade teacher *did* play an important role in her life. None of the answer choices make sense because they don't have anything to do with how Beverly's seventh-grade teacher's influenced her. Remember that Beverly's *first-grade* teacher put her in the lowest reading group.

15 C Read the seventh paragraph again. The seventh paragraph tells how many copies Beverly Cleary's books have sold. Consider which of the questions stated in the answer choices this information answers. Get rid of **A**, **B**, and **D** because the answers to these questions are given in other paragraphs. The correct answer choice is **C**.

MAKING MAPLE SYRUP

16 G Read the first paragraph. The first paragraph states that Noel is wearing a scarf and mittens. This indicates that it is cold outside. Get rid of **F**, **H**, and **J** because wearing a scarf and mittens doesn't tell anything about making maple syrup, learning how to tap a tree, or Noel's grade in school. The correct answer choice is **G**.

17 B This question asks about the purpose of the second and third paragraphs. The second and third paragraphs provide information about gathering sap for maple syrup. Get rid of **A** because information about gathering sap does not describe Noel and his mother. Cross off **C** because information about collecting sap does not encourage readers. Get rid of **D** too because information about collecting sap does not contrast sap and sugar. The correct answer choice is **B** because information about collecting sap in the early spring *does* explain why Noel and his mother are in the woods in the cold.

18 G Read the end of the passage. The last paragraph says that Noel will savor eating the maple syrup because he knows how hard it was to make. From this, you can infer that he is excited about eating the maple syrup but also patient. Get rid of **F**, **H**, and **J** because the description doesn't support the conclusion that Noel is cold but happy, sad and tired, or hurried and greedy. The correct answer choice is **G**.

19 D Consider which answer choice best supports the inference that Noel and his mother are working in the woods in late March. Get rid of **A** because it doesn't provide any information about what time of year Noel and his mom are working. Cross off **B** and **C** because they don't discuss Noel and his mother or the time of year. Answer choice **D** tells about the last remains of snow, which indicates late March. That means answer choice **D** is correct. It supports the inference that Noel and his mother are working in late March.

20 H The story says that Noel and his mother spend the day moving from tree to tree, inserting taps into the trees. That helps you get rid of **F**, **G**, and **J**. The correct answer choice is **H**.

21 B This question asks you to figure out why the passage is interesting and educational. A passage may be interesting, but it is only educational when it tells information about a real thing. Consider each answer choice. Get rid of **A** because the recipes are not provided. Cross off **C** because the passage doesn't encourage people to eat maple syrup. The passage *does* portray maple syrup as something that Noel enjoys eating, but that's not educational. Also get rid of **D** because parents and children working together is interesting but not educational. Answer choice **B** is correct because the passage *does* tell a story about a real activity. The story is interesting, and the information about the real activity is educational.

22 J Consider what each of the paragraphs listed in the answer choices tells you. Get rid of **F** because the sixth paragraph is about how much sap each tree makes and how much sap is needed to make maple syrup. This is not about the history of maple syrup. Cross off **G** because the fifth paragraph is about the process Noel and his mother use to collect sap and make maple syrup. This is not about the history of maple syrup. Get rid of **H** because the fourth paragraph is about the factors that affect the quality and quantity of sap produced by a maple tree. This is not about the history of maple syrup. Answer choice **J** is correct because the second paragraph tells about the Native American custom of making maple syrup a long time ago. That is about the history of maple syrup.

23 C This question asks you about the sixth paragraph. The sixth paragraph tells you that you need 35 gallons of sap to make one gallon of maple syrup. Consider which of the questions stated in the answer choices this information answers. Get rid of **A**, **B**, and **D** because these questions are not answered by the information in the sixth paragraph. The correct answer choice is **C**.

24 G Find the word "dribbled" in the seventh paragraph. Replace the word "dribbled" with the words in the answer choices to see which fits the best. Get rid of **F** because "washed over waffles" doesn't make sense. Cross off **H** because "mixed over waffles" doesn't make sense either. **J**, "bounced over waffles," doesn't make sense. The correct answer choice is **G** because "poured over waffles" makes sense.

25 D Use information in the story to decide why the Native American girl stopped her pony. Read the third and fourth paragraphs. The story states that the Native American girl stopped because she heard Henrique's stomach and wanted to feed Henrique. Get rid of **A**, **B**, and **C**. The Native American girl heard Henrique's hunger, which means she could tell that Henrique was in trouble and couldn't find food. Therefore, the correct answer choice is **D**.

26 G Find the part of the story in which Henrique and the Native American girl reach the Native Gardens. Look for important information that could show how Henrique felt. She smiles at her new friend. That means you can get rid of **F**, **H**, and **J** because Henrique doesn't act frightened, unsure, or like she doesn't want to go home. The correct answer choice is **G**.

27 D The third paragraph states that Henrique is lost and frightened when she first sees the Native American girl. Get rid of **A** because this paragraph is not about the buffalo. Cross out **B** because this paragraph is not about myths or dreams. Get rid of **C** because Henrique is hungry in this paragraph. The correct answer choice is **D** because Henrique is tired and hungry as a result of not eating before she left home. Therefore, she probably wishes she had never left home.

28 H Henrique leaves her house In the beginning of the story. Therefore, you should quickly read, or skim, the beginning of the story for the name of the place that Henrique is headed. Get rid of **F**, **G**, and **J**. The correct answer choice is H.

29 A Find the word "anguish" in the sixth paragraph. Read story looking for clues, such as "so weak" and "thunder of your stomach." Decide which makes the most sense. Get rid of **B** and **C** because life and happiness do not make sense. Henrique was weak and hungry. Cross out **D** because the Native American girl heard the sounds of Henrique's hungry stomach. Although Henrique may have been sad, the Native American girl heard the sounds of Henrique's stomach, not her sadness. The correct answer choice is **A** because Henrique's stomach was making pained sounds.

30 J This question asks you where you could find another story similar to "The Great Rift." Get rid of **F**, **G**, and **H** because a dictionary, a reference book, and a history do not contain stories. They contain facts. Therefore, the correct answer choice must be **J**.

31 A This question asks about the author's purpose. Get rid of **B** because the author does not describe the life of pioneers in detail. Cross out **C** because the author does not tell how to find the Native Gardens. Get rid of **D** because the author does not tell a scary story. Therefore, the correct answer choice is **A**. The author *does* tell a mysterious story about the Great Rift.

32 H This question asks you to identify the answer choice question that is *not* answered by the first paragraph. The first paragraph tells why Henrique wandered away from her cabin, so **F** isn't right. The first paragraph tells what Henrique's dolls were made of, so **G** is incorrect. It also tells you that she was collecting pinecones as she walked. That makes **J** incorrect. Henrique stops walking because she was feeling weak and hungry. But we don't learn that until the *second* paragraph! The correct answer choice is **H**.

33 C This question asks you to identify what the Native American girl did as a result of Henrique forgetting to eat. Get rid of **A**, **B**, and **D** because the Native American girl didn't do any of these things. **C** is correct because the Native American girl had Henrique travel on her horse to find the Native Gardens and eat.

ISLAND LIFE

34 H This question asks you to identify what it means to skim an article. Skimming means to read quickly in order to find the main ideas. Therefore, the correct answer choice is **H**.

35 B This question asks you to figure out the conclusion supported by the article. Get rid of **A** because the article says that there are no phone lines and the family has to use cell phones. It is *not* true that they prefer to use phone lines. Cross out **C** because the article does not say that steamers are more difficult to find than other types of clams. Get rid of **D** because the article states that most people live on Obstruction Island in the summer only. The correct answer choice is **B** because the article says that the family has to take a boat to go grocery shopping. That supports the conclusion that the family has to take a lot of time for grocery shopping.

36 H In the word "unfortunately," the "un" is a prefix that means "not." Therefore, "unfortunately" means "not fortunately." To answer this question, you have to find the word in which "un" is also used to mean "not." Get rid of **F, G,** and **J** because the "un" does not mean "not" in the words "funny," "uncle," and "under." The correct answer choice is **H** because the "un" means "not" in the word "unwise." ("Unwise" means "not wise.")

37 D This question asks you about the purpose of the poem. The poem describes how much the author likes living on an island. Get rid of **A** because the poem doesn't mention the author's father. The poem is also about how the author does not feel lonely. Cross out **B** and **C** because the poem doesn't mention anything about writing poetry at school or singing poems on a boat ride. The correct answer choice is **D** because the poem explains how the author feels about living on an island.

38 G Find the part of the story where the narrator describes finding clams. The eighth paragraph states that the narrator and Jenny find out when there will be a low tide and more of the beach will be exposed. Get rid of **F, H,** and **J**. The correct answer choice is **G**.

39 D The best way to answer questions about specific information is to skim the selection. Don't bother trying to memorize. You always have time to find the answer. Find the paragraph that describes the narrator and Jenny looking for clams. What do they do after checking the tide charts and before looking for water spurts? They gather the shovels and buckets. Therefore, answer choice **D** is correct.

40 J From what the story tells you, you know that the island is off the coast of Washington. Therefore, you need to look at the map and find the state of Washington. Now, identify the state that is directly south of Washington. The correct answer choice is **J**, Oregon.

THE DOOR IN THE CLOSET

41 C Consider the descriptions. Both "angry day" and "clouds spit hard" refer to the weather. These descriptions portray the weather as being very harsh. Get rid of **A** because the descriptions do not discuss the temperature. Cross off **B** because the descriptions do not convey the mood of a child. Eliminate **D** because the descriptions do not provide information about the time of year either. Therefore, you know the correct answer is **C**.

42 F Go back to the poem and find the part in which the narrator squeezes through the door. After the narrator squeezed through the door, the narrator says that he or she could barely believe what he or she saw. Consider which answer choice is best supported by this information from the poem. Get rid of **G**, **H**, and **J** because the narrator does not seem to be bored, upset, or anxious. The correct answer choice is **F** because the narrator seems to be surprised.

43 D Consider your overall impression of the narrator in this poem. Describe the narrator in your own words. Now consider the answer choices, and identify the answer choice that most closely matches your description. Get rid of **A**. Although the narrator does seem happy about finding a place full of candy, the narrator is bored for most of the poem because of the rain. Cross off **B**. Although the narrator is excited about the candy, he or she never shows hunger. Get rid of **C** because the narrator is not cranky. Although the narrator is bored from the rain, the narrator is interested in the small door in the closet. The correct answer choice is **D** because the narrator is curious in the poem.

44 F Consider the words listed in the question. Get rid of **G** because the word "paused" does not support a feeling of excitement. Cross off **H** because the word "unsure" does not support a feeling of confidence. Eliminate **J** because the word "blinked" does not support a feeling of sleepiness. The correct answer choice is **F**, doubt, because all the words listed support a feeling of doubt.

45 B At the end of the poem, the poet wakes up in bed and the door is gone. Consider how this would make you feel. At the end of the poem, it was hard to tell if the events were real or part of a dream. Get rid of **F** because the reader would probably not feel full or satisfied from being unexpectedly pulled out of a candy-filled dream. Eliminate **C** because the reader would probably not feel restless and adventurous after such interesting events. Cross off **D** because the reader would not feel disgusted with the child in the poem. The correct answer choice is **B** because the reader would most likely feel mystified by the events.

46 F This question asks you to identify the main idea of the poem. Consider what the poem was mainly about. Get rid of **G** because the friendly stranger was a detail in the poem—not the main idea. Cross off **H** because only one line in the poem refers to the possibility of candy making you sick. That makes this is a detail, not the main idea either. Get rid of **J** because the information in the poem does not support the idea that it should rain more often. The correct answer choice is **F** because the poem is mainly about a dream that seems real.

47 C Find the word "fast" in the ninth line. Read the poem for context clues that tell the meaning of the word. The poem says that the door "creaked as I pushed with all my might." Therefore, you know that the door was hard to open. Now replace the word fast in the ninth line with each of the answer choices. Decide which answer choice makes the most sense. Get rid of **A** because "the closet held alert" does not make sense. Cross off **B** because "the closet held quick" does not make sense. Eliminate **D** because "the closet held open" is the opposite of what happened. The correct answer choice is **C** because "the closet door held secure" fits perfectly.

48 G In lines 24 through 27, the author describes the candy world. Get rid of **F** because the author's description does not provide the reader with instructions for growing coconut grass. Cross off **H**. Although the poem does rhyme and the setting is a rainy day, these lines are not about the author giving the reader a rhyme. These lines describe a candy world. Get rid of **J** because the author's description does not provide the reader with an understanding of chickens. The correct answer choice is **G** because the author's description provides a picture of a magical world.

49 B In the word "opened," the "ed" shows that the word is in the past tense. To answer this question, you want to find the word in which "ed" is also used to mean the past tense form of a verb. Get rid of **A**, **C**, and **D** because the "ed" does not indicate the past tense form of a verb in the words educate, deed, and meddle. The correct answer choice is **B** because the "ed" indicates the past tense form of the word "dance."

50 H The line "I thought I fell into a storybook" is an example of figurative language. Figurative language always has a symbolic meaning, so you can get rid of the answers that seem to be too literal, such as **F** and **J**. The narrator didn't *actually* fall into anything! The narrator simply felt that the candy world was so wonderful and unbelievable that it had to be like a storybook. That makes **H** the best answer choice.

51 A This question asks you to identify the author's purpose. Get rid of **B** because this poem does not explain the meaning of dreams. Cross off **C** because this poem does not discourage children from eating too many sweets. Eliminate **D** because this poem does not persuade children to explore their closets. This poem does not explain anything to the reader or try to convince the reader of anything. The correct answer choice is **A** because the poem does tell an amusing story about imagination.

52 J This question asks you to identify the reason that the door in the closet is gone at the end of the poem. Get rid of **F** because the poem states that the narrator checked the closet and did not find the door. Therefore, the poet did not forget about it. Cross out **G** because the poem states that the door could not be found. Therefore, it doesn't matter if the door was locked. Get rid of **H** because the poem does not give any information to support the idea that the poet moved to another house. The correct answer choice is **J** because the poem states that the narrator was back in bed. Therefore, this supports the idea that the candy world was a dream.

PRACTICE TEST #2
ANSWERS AND
EXPLANATIONS

LEARNING AN ANCIENT GAME

1   **C**   Find the paragraph that has information that could best be described by the heading "Proper Footwear." Get rid of **A** because paragraph 1 is about Tyson watching television. Cross off **B** because paragraph 4 is about the history of bowling. Get rid of **D** because paragraph 7 is about Tyson's first and second try. The correct answer choice is **C**. Paragraph 6 is about bowling shoes.

2   **F**   Skim the beginning of the passage, and look for key words about Malcolm's attitude toward Tyson. Some key words are "annoyance" and "surprised." Get rid of **G** because Malcolm speaks to his son in a scolding way in the beginning of passage. Therefore, Malcolm is neither quiet nor proud. Cross off **H**. Although Malcolm is surprised, he is not delighted to find his son watching television. Get rid of **J** because Malcolm is neither excited nor calm. The best answer choice is **F**. Malcolm's annoyance could be described as frustrated, and his surprise could be described as shock.

3   **C**   This question asks you to identify how the author made the subject of bowling more interesting. The author includes information about bowling within a simple story about a father and son playing it. Get rid of **A** because the author does not give advice about bowling. Cross off **B** because the author does not tell an exciting story about a family. Get rid of **D** too. Although the author *does* show the father as being annoyed in the beginning of the passage, the father's anger does not make bowling more interesting. Also, the father's anger occurs only in the beginning of the passage, not throughout. The correct answer choice is **C**.

4   **J**   Skim the passage to find information about the word bowling. The passage states that the word bowling might have come from the Saxon word *bolla* and the Danish word *bolle*. Eliminate **F**, **G**, and **H**. The correct answer choice is **J**.

5   **B**   This question asks you to find what part of the passage supports the inference that people have bowled for more than 7,000 years. Get rid of **A** because the weight and sizes of a bowling ball do not support the inference. Cross out **C** because Tyson's bowling attempts do not support the inference. Get rid of **D** because bowling equipment used years ago does not support the inference either. The correct answer choice is **B**. Information about the age of ancient bowling pins supports the inference.

6 F This question asks you to identify the author's purpose in writing the first three paragraphs. Skim these paragraphs. They are about Malcolm being annoyed about Tyson watching television and about them planning to go bowling. Get rid of **G** because the author's purpose in these paragraphs is not to explain why Malcolm enjoys bowling. Cross off **H** because the author's purpose in these paragraphs is not to encourage people to bowl. Get rid of **J** because the author's purpose in these paragraphs is not to discuss the history of bowling. The correct answer choice is **F**. The author *does* provide a human angle on the topic of bowling.

7 A Skim the final paragraph for clues, such as "With time, he will become a better bowler." Get rid of **B**, **C**, and **D** because the final paragraph does not provide information about Tyson's father's bowling skills, Malcolm and Tyson buying special bowling shoes, or Tyson watching television when he gets home. The correct answer choice is **A** because the last paragraph supports the conclusion that Tyson will go bowling again.

8 H Skim paragraph 6 and identify context clues that indicate the meaning of the word "slick," such as "leather" and "slide." Find the word "slick" and replace it with each of the answer choices to identify which answer choice makes the most sense. Get rid of **F** because "sly" doesn't really make sense. Cross off **G** because a "fancy" sole wouldn't necessarily enable a bowler to slide. Eliminate **J** because it doesn't make sense to describe leather as "fast." The correct answer choice is **H**, because a smooth sole enables the bowler to slide. That makes the most sense.

9 D Skim Paragraph 5. Paragraph 5 provides information about bowling equipment, such as the pins, bowling lane, and bowling ball. Get rid of **A**, **B**, and **C** because this paragraph doesn't talk about strikes, Malcolm's frustration, or when bowling was invented. The correct answer choice is **D**. This paragraph provides information about the weight of tenpins.

10 J   Skim paragraph 6. Get rid of **F, G,** and **H** because nothing in paragraph 6 says how long Lewis waters the garden, if Lewis naps in the garden, or how many grapefruit were growing on trees. The paragraph lists the kind of plants growing in the garden. Therefore, the correct answer choice is **J**.

11 C   Locate the underlined word "wash" in the eighth paragraph. Look for context clues in the eighth paragraph, such as "natural path." Now replace the word "wash" with each answer choice in order to see which answer choice makes the most sense. Get rid of **A** because laundry is not a natural path. Cross off **B** because a pool is not a natural path. Eliminate **D** because clean clothes are not a natural path. The correct answer choice is **C** because a riverbed could be a natural path. "Lewis headed out to the riverbed" makes sense.

12 H   This question asks you to identify the sentence that informs you that the passage is historical fiction. Therefore, you need to identify the sentence that shows that this passage occurred in the distant past. Get rid of **F, G,** and **J** because these answer choices do not indicate a distant past. The correct answer choice is **H** because people commonly listened to adventure stories on the radio in the distant past. This is not something that people commonly do today.

13 A   This question asks you to find the description that does *not* contribute to the idea that Lewis was scared when he was in the wash. Get rid of **B** because Grandpa warned Lewis about the danger of being in the wash while it rained. Therefore, this description contributes to the idea of Lewis feeling scared. Cross off **C** because Lewis was scared of being in the wash while it rained. As a result, Lewis turned around when it began to rain. Therefore, this description also contributes to the idea of Lewis feeling scared. Get rid of **D**. Lewis fell and skinned his knee because he was rushing out of the wash as a result of his fear. Therefore, this description contributes to the idea of Lewis feeling scared. The correct answer choice is **A** because the description of Lewis not feeling the raindrops does *not* contribute to the idea of Lewis feeling fear.

14 F   Read the part of the passage that describes Lewis tripping in the wash. The passage states that Lewis turned to look back because he wanted to make sure that water wasn't rushing toward him. Get rid of **G** and **H** because Lewis didn't trip on his shoelace or hurry so his grandpa wouldn't get mad. Cross off **J** because it had been raining for a while before Lewis tripped. Therefore, Lewis didn't trip because he knew it had started raining. The correct answer choice is **F**. Lewis was worried about getting swept down the wash. Therefore, he turned to look back, didn't see the boulder in front of him, and tripped.

15 C This question asks you to tell what the story is mostly about. Get rid of **A** because Lewis's pet lizard Liza is only a detail in the story. It is not what the story is mostly about. Cross off **B** because the story contains details about a rock garden, not a flower garden. Therefore, this answer choice presents an inaccurate detail from the story. Get rid of **D** because the story has details about how Lewis is happy to spend the summer in the desert. Therefore, this answer choice gives an inaccurate detail from the story. The correct answer choice is **C**. A lot of the story focuses on how Lewis feels love for his grandparents. Therefore, this is what the story is mainly about.

16 H Skim the end of the story in which Lewis returns to the house with scrapes. Look for clues, such as "lump in his throat" and "hugged his grandpa." Get rid of **F** because Lewis is not adventurous when he returns to his grandparents' house. Cross off **G** because Lewis may be safe, but he is still wet from the rain. (He is not dry.) Get rid of **J** because Lewis may be disappointed, but it is not well supported by the story. The correct answer choice is **H**. The information in the story supports the description of Lewis as upset but relieved.

17 A Skim paragraph 2. Get rid of **B**, **C**, and **D** because there is no information in paragraph 2 about what is growing in the cactus garden, where Grandma Juanita is, and why Lewis went to the wash. The paragraph mentions that Lewis will start sixth grade in the fall. Therefore, the correct answer choice is **A**.

18 G Find the underlined word "diamond" in the seventh paragraph. Look for context clues, such as "outfield" and "home plate." In addition to using context clues, you should also replace the word "diamond" with each answer choice in order to see which answer choice makes the most sense. Get rid of **F** because "fast on the cutter" doesn't make sense. Cross off **H** because "fast on the shape" doesn't make sense. Eliminate **J** because "fast on the gem" doesn't make sense. The correct answer choice is **G**, because "fast on the field" makes the most sense.

19 B This question asks you to identify the fact that supports the inference that Roberto Clemente was a great baseball player. Get rid of **A** because Roberto Clemente's birthplace does not support this. Cross off **C** because Roberto Clemente working hard delivering milk does not support this. Eliminate **D** because Roberto Clemente helping children learn baseball does not support this inference. Answer choice **B** is correct. The fact that Roberto Clemente got 3,000 hits supports the inference that he was a great baseball player.

20 H Paragraph 7 describes Clemente's skill as a baseball player. Get rid of **F** because paragraph 7 is not about the beginning of Clemente's career. Cross off **G** because paragraph 7 is not about the end of Clement's career or about his humility. Eliminate **J** because paragraph 7 is not about Clemente's respect for his parents. Paragraph 7 is about how Clemente had miraculous skill as a baseball player. It is likely that his skill wowed fans. Therefore, the correct answer choice is **H**.

21 D This question asks you to identify the author's purpose. You need to consider what the passage did. This passage described the details from Roberto Clemente's life. Get rid of **A** because the passage did not describe how to be a spray hitter. Cross off **B** because the passage did not provide a history of baseball. Eliminate **C**. Although the passage may have made the reader feel sad when sad moments in Roberto Clemente's life were described, the passage also noted happy moments from Roberto Clemente's life. The correct answer choice is **D** because the passage did offer biographical information.

22 H The fifth paragraph is about the beginning of Clemente's pro-baseball career in the United States. Get rid of **F, G,** and **J** because you find out about Clemente's family and values, community service, and career highlights in other paragraphs. The best description of paragraph 5, the correct answer choice, is **H**, American Introduction.

23 D This question asks you to identify which question is answered in paragraph 9. Paragraph 9 describes the end of Clemente's life. Get rid of **A**, **B**, and **C** because how many hits Clemente got, when he signed with the Dodgers, and who Clemente played for after the Dodgers are answered in other paragraphs. Paragraph 9 stated the year that Clemente died. Therefore, the correct answer choice is **D**.

24 G Find the term "spray hitter" in the passage. Information about being a spray hitter is found in the eighth paragraph. The eighth paragraph states that a spray hitter is someone that hits the ball all over the field. Get rid of **F**, **H**, and **J** because a spray hitter is not someone that swings the bat quickly, hits softly and lightly, or goes to bat when another player is sick. The correct answer choice is **G**.

MENG CHIANG-NU'S JOURNEY

25 C Find the word "expired" in the passage, and then look for surrounding context clues. After Meng Chiang-nu finds out that her husband expired, she faints and wakes up sobbing. Replace the word "expired" with each of the answer choices in order to identify which answer choice makes the most sense. Get rid of **A** because it does not make sense that Meng Chiang-nu would faint upon finding out that her husband breathed. Cross off **B** because "had outdated while working to build the wall" doesn't make sense. Eliminate **D** because Meng Chiang-nu wouldn't be upset if her husband laughed. The correct answer choice is **C**, because "had died while working to build the wall" makes the most sense.

26 F The end of the fifth paragraph says that the emperor was overwhelmed by Meng Chiang-nu's beauty. In the sixth paragraph, you know that the emperor asked Meng Chiang-nu to marry him. Therefore, answer choice **F** is correct. Remember that the emperor doesn't know Meng Chaing-nu will turn into a fish yet.

27 A Locate the place in the story where Meng Chiang-nu begins crying. The story states that she began crying after finding out that her husband has died. Get rid of **B**, **C**, and **D** because the passage does not state that the workers frightened her, that the winter clothes were stolen, or that she was angry at the wall being built. Answer choice **A** is correct.

28 H This question asks you to consider the author's purpose. Get rid of **F** and **J**. Although you may want to visit the Great Wall after reading this story, the author focuses this story on Meng Chiang-nu, not on the Great Wall. Cross off **G**. Although it may be adventurous that Meng Chiang-nu decided to travel to the wall to find her husband, the author described both the adventurous actions and regular actions of Meng Chiang-nu. The author tells the story of Meng Chiang-nu and how she became a colorful fish. Therefore, answer choice **H** is correct.

29 C When Meng Chiang-nu agrees to marry the emperor, she asks for two things: that her husband be buried in a gold coffin and that the emperor attend the wedding. Get rid of **A**, **B**, and **D** because Meng Chiang-nu did not ask the emperor to become a fish, give her a gold bracelet, or promise to tear down the wall in exchange for the promise of marriage. The correct answer choice is **C**.

30 G This question asks you to identify the question that is *not* answered by the information in the first and second paragraphs. These paragraphs state that the emperor was building the Great Wall to protect his kingdom. They also tell that Meng Chiang-nu's husband was named Wan Hsi-liang and that Meng Chiang-nu was upset because her husband had to leave to work on the Wall. Get rid of **F**, **H**, and **J** because these questions can be answered by the information in these paragraphs. The correct answer choice is **G** because these paragraphs do *not* contain information about why Meng Chiang-nu had not heard from her husband.

31 D In order to identify the correct answer choice, you need to figure out that this story is a myth. You know it's a myth because it describes something happened a long time ago and is probably not real. Get rid of **A**, because this story is not a poem. Cross off **B** because this story does not contain geographical information similar to an entry on an atlas. Eliminate **C** because this story does not focus only on the wall. It also focuses on characters. A book about different walls would only focus on the walls. The correct answer choice is **D** because this story is a myth. Therefore, you could find a similar story in a collection of myths.

32 H The best way to find information in a selection conveniently is to skim. Therefore, the correct answer choice is **H**. The actions listed in **F**, **G**, or **J** are not good ways to find information in a selection.

33 A Before Meng Chiang-nu is supposed to marry the emperor, she slips into the river and becomes a fish. Get rid **B, C,** and **D** because Meng Chiang-nu does not show appreciation, delight, or gratitude toward the emperor when she slips into the river and becomes a fish. It is *most likely* that Meng Chiang-nu dislikes the emperor for playing a role in her husband's death.

34 H For this question, you need to use the description in the story to make an inference. As you learned in one of the lessons, the key to answering questions about figurative language is not to take them literally. The passage states that the people were "starving." Therefore, the people were probably very thin. Get rid of **F, G,** and **J.** The correct answer choice is **H.**

35 C Use the information in the graph to answer this question. Get rid of **A** because Meng Chiang-nu walked twelve miles on the fourth day, sixteen miles on the first day, and ten miles on the second day. Therefore, she did not walk more miles on the fourth day than on the first or second day. Cross off **B** because she walked twelve miles on the fourth day, ten miles on the second day, and six miles on the third day. Therefore, she did not walk fewer miles on the fourth day than the second or third day. Eliminate **D** because she walked ten miles on the second day, sixteen miles on the first day, and six miles on the third day. Therefore, she did not walk more miles on the second day than on either the first or third day. The correct answer choice is **B** because she walked sixteen miles on the first day. She walked sixteen miles on the second and third day combined. Therefore, she walked as many miles on the first day as on the second and third days combined.

Making Money

36 G In the word filling, the "ing" shows that the action is in the process of happening. To answer this question, you want to find the word in which "ing" is also used to mean an action that is in the process of happening. Get rid of **F, H,** and **J** because the "ing" does not indicate that an action is happening. The correct answer choice is **G.**

37 C This question asks you to identify the author's purpose in lines 9 through 12. In these lines, the author describes what Matthew and Scott are like. Get rid of **A** because the author's description does not help the reader to come up with ideas to make money. Cross off **B** because the author's description does not help the reader to feel sorry for the worms. Eliminate **D** because the author's description does not help the reader to learn how the boys plan to get rich. The author describes the boys as "greedy." This description helps the reader to develop an understanding of the characters. Therefore, the correct answer choice is **C**.

38 H Consider the descriptions. "Slimy," "slithering," "muddy," and "soggy" all refer to the worms and the earth that the worms are in negatively. Get rid of **F, G,** and **J** because these descriptions do not provide a feeling about the creativity of the boys, the size of the shed, or the time of the year. These descriptions provide a negative feeling about worms. Therefore, the correct answer choice is **H**.

39 D Find the part of the poem in which the boys can't sell their worms and look for clues that indicate the boys' feeling, such as "losing all heart." This description does not support the idea that the boys feel hopeful, angry, or energetic. Therefore, get rid of **A, B,** and **C**. This description does support the idea that the boys feel discouraged. Therefore, the correct answer choice is **D**.

40 H This question asks you to identify the *best* description of the two boys in the poem. Get rid of **F** and **G** because the poem states that the boys are "greedy" and they leave the worms to die in the barrel. These are not innocent or considerate characteristics. Cross out **J** because the poem states, "they're not very bright." Therefore, the boys are not smart. The correct answer choice is **H** because the leaving the worms in the barrel could *best* be described as thoughtless.

41 A First, answer this question in your own words. How do these words make you feel? The words listed in the question seem spooky. Get rid of **B, C,** and **D** because the words do not create a feeling of optimism, happiness, or anger. The correct answer choice is **A** because these words create a spooky feeling, or a feeling of fright.

42 H Read lines 13 through 16. These lines list the ways that the boys try to come up with more money. These lines state that the boys come up with crazy schemes, like trying to sell broken toys and old books. Think about how these lines make you feel. Come up with the answer in your own words then consider each answer choice. Get rid of **F** because a reader would probably not feel envious of crazy schemes. Although a reader might feel confused about why the boys think they can make money selling broken games, a reader would probably not feel angry. Cross out **G**. Although the boys' schemes do not make the most sense, they are "crazy" schemes and certainly not boring. Eliminate **J**. The correct answer choice is **H**. The idea of that the boys think they can make money selling each other is amusing.

43 D This question asks you to identify the conclusion that is supported by the information in the poem. Get rid of **A**, **B**, and **C** because the poem does not include information about worms being important to the well-being of the earth, the boys becoming businessmen in the future, or parents giving money to their children. The poem does describe the worms as creepy. But it also suggests that the worms should be treated with respect in the last stanza. Therefore, answer choice **D** is correct.

44 H This poem asks you to identify a word with the same meaning as "dough" in the poem. Look for context clues indicating the meaning of the word "dough" in the poem, such as "fill their pockets" and "money." Replace the word "dough" with each of the answer choices and decide which answer choice makes the most sense. Get rid of **F** because "fill their pockets with lots of paste" doesn't make sense. Cross out **G** because "fill their pockets with lots of batter" doesn't make sense. Eliminate **J** because "fill their pockets with lots of pulp" doesn't make sense. "Fill their pockets with lots of money" does make sense and is supported by the context clues. Therefore, answer choice **H** is correct.

45 B It helps to get rid of wrong answer choices for this question. Which statement is supported by what you read in this essay? Do you know that Grandpa Henry owned a bakery in Germany? No, so **A** must be wrong. The story says that Grandpa Henry looked like a ghost when covered in flour, but a real ghost didn't haunt the bakery. That makes **C** a wrong answer choice. **D** is wrong because the bakery sells many different things. According to the essay, Grandma Jenny got hungry for a slice of Black Forest cake; from then on, Henry's bakery started selling deserts. That makes answer choice **B** correct.

46 J Skimming means reading quickly. The makes **J** the correct answer choice. Remember the meaning of skimming, and you'll always answer questions like these correctly.

47 B We are told in the story that Grandpa Henry came from Germany. Look at the map and find Germany in the center. Now look for the country that is directly north of Germany. Look up on the map. There you will find the right answer. It is the country of Denmark. That makes **B** the correct answer choice.

48 G The "ly" in the word crumbly is a suffix that turns the word "crumb" into "with crumbs." "Nicely" means "with niceness," the "ly" does the same thing as in the word "crumbly." None of the words in the other answer choices—"lying," "folly," or "lyric"—use their "ly" in the same way. The correct answer is **G**.

49 A The story says the narrator's mother didn't want to leave for the hospital until she removed a batch of almond cookies from the oven. That suggests the mother wanted to finish baking cookies, which makes **A** the correct answer choice. **B** is a close second choice, but **A** fits better. The narrator didn't need to grease the muffin tins, so **C** isn't right. We are also never told that the family could not afford to go to a hospital, so **D** is not the correct answer choice either.

50 J Look at the five circles from the question, and try to figure out which step is missing. Think about the directions for making muffins. What happens after you mix the ingredients and before you bake them? Read the story again for the directions if you want to. Adding almonds is not part of the directions, so you can safely get rid of **F**. And you can't allow the muffins to cool until after they're baked, so throw out **G**. The story also tells us that you cut the butter into the flour when you mix the ingredients, so you can cross of **H**. That leaves **J** as the best answer choice.

51 A The poem at the beginning of the article lists many different baked goods. That means that its purpose is probably to give you a sense of the many things that are made at the bakery. We don't know if bakers sing to their bread because it helps it rise, so **B** is wrong. The story also doesn't say if Grandpa Henry sang as he baked, so **C** is not the best answer choice. **D** is also wrong because the story doesn't say anything about the first poem that the author ever memorized.

52 J This story is mainly about the author's family and their bakery. There's nothing sad about the story. It's not really just about a child and his or her grandfather. The author doesn't invite people to the bakery or offer a recipe, which rules out **G** and **H**. The best answer choice is **J**. The author probably wrote the story to tell about the family and their bakery business.

COOL BOOKS FOR COOL READERS

The more you read, the better you get at it. But reading stories, novels, and poetry will help you do much more than do better in school. You can read for fun and for escape. You can also find out about the lives of children like yourself who have grown up in places, cultures, or time periods different from your own. It's just like going on a trip, except that you don't have to worry about the driving.

The following list includes books recommended by teachers, librarians, and—most importantly—other children. Check out the books in your library, and take home the ones that seem interesting to you. If you like a book, you can ask your parents, friends, teacher, or librarian to recommend others like it. If you like a book, but it's too hard for you, ask a parent to read it to you. But if you're not hooked after you've read a few chapters of a book, don't worry about it. Try something else. Nobody's grading you!

Babbitt, Natalie. *Tuck Everlasting.* (Fantasy)

Baum, Frank L. *The Wizard of Oz.* (Fantasy)

Blume, Judy. *Just As Long As We're Together.* (Contemporary Fiction) *Here's to You, Rachel Robinson* is the sequel to this book. Blume has written many other popular books for young people, including *Tales of a Fourth Grade Nothing,* the first in a series about Peter Hatcher and his little brother, Fudge.

Burnett, Frances Hodgson. *The Secret Garden.* (Classic)

Carroll, Lewis. *Alice's Adventures in Wonderland.* (Classic) Alice's adventures continue in *Through the Looking Glass.*

Cleary, Beverly. *Beezus and Ramona.* (Contemporary Fiction) This book begins Cleary's series about Ramona Quimby. This story is told from the point of view of Ramona's older sister, Beezus.

Dahl, Roald. *James and the Giant Peach.* (Fantasy)
Other favorite books by Dahl include *Charlie and the Chocolate Factory, Matilda,* and *Fantastic Mr. Fox.*

Danziger, Paula. *The Cat Ate My Gymsuit.* (Contemporary Fiction)
Also try Danziger's series about Amber Brown, which begins with *Amber Brown is Not a Crayon.*

Dorris, Michael. *Guests.* (Contemporary Fiction)

Erdrich, Louise. *The Birchbark House.* (Historical Fiction)

Farley, *The Black Stallion.* (Classic)
The Black Stallion Returns is the next book in Farley's series about the magnificent stallion, Black.

Fitzhugh, Louise. *Harriet the Spy.* (Contemporary Fiction)

Fleischman, Paul. *Seedfolks.* (Contemporary Fiction)

Gipson, Fred. *Old Yeller.* (Classic)

Grahame, Kenneth. *The Wind in the Willows.* (Classic)

Konigsburg, E. L. *From the Mixed-Up Files of Mrs. Basil E. Frankweiler.* (Contemporary Fiction)

L'Engle, Madeleine. *A Wrinkle in Time.* (Science Fiction, Contemporary Fiction)
L'Engle's series about the Murry family continues in *A Swiftly Tilting Planet, A Wind in the Door,* and *Many Waters.* Also try *A Ring of Endless Light,* a favorite in her series about Vicky Austin and her family.

Lewis, C. S. *The Lion, the Witch, and the Wardrobe.* (Classic, Fantasy)
The first book in the *Chronicles of Narnia.*

King-Smith, Dick. *Babe, the Gallant Pig.* (Fantasy)

Lowry, Lois. *Number the Stars.* (Historical Fiction)

Mead, Alice. *Junebug.* (Contemporary Fiction)

Myers, Walter Dean. *Me, Mop, and the Moondance Kid.* (Contemporary Fiction)

MacLachlan, Patricia. *Sarah, Plain and Tall.* (Historical Fiction)

Namioka, Lensey. *Yang the Youngest and His Terrible Ear.* (Contemporary Fiction)

Norton, Mary. *The Borrowers.* (Fantasy)

O'Brien, Robert C. *Mrs. Frisby and the Rats of NIMH.* (Fantasy)

O'Dell, Scott. *Island of the Blue Dolphins.* (Historical Fiction)

Pullman, Philip. *Firework-Maker's Daughter.* (Fantasy)
For a worthwhile challenge, try Pullman's fantasy *The Golden Compass* and its sequel, *The Subtle Knife.*

Paterson, Katherine. *Bridge to Terabithia. (Contemporary Fiction)*
Other popular books by Paterson include *The Great Gilly Hopkins, The Master Puppeteer,* and *The King's Equal,* an original fairy tale.

Rowling, J. K. *Harry Potter and the Sorcerer's Stone.* (Fantasy)
The first in a wildly popular series of fantasy books that includes *Harry Potter and the Chamber of Secrets, Harry Potter and the Prisoner of Azkaban,* and *Harry Potter and the Goblet of Fire.*

de Saint-Exupery, Antoine. *The Little Prince.* (Classic)

Scieszka, Jon. *Summer Reading Is Killing Me!* (Humor)
Scieszka has written many other funny books for children. Try *Stinky Cheese Man and Other Fairly Stupid Tales* and *Knights of the Kitchen Table.*

Selden, George. *The Cricket in Times Square.* (Classic)

Silverstein, Shel. *Where the Sidewalk Ends.* (Poetry)
Silverstein has written two other books of humorous poetry: *A Light in the Attic* and *Falling Up.*

Sobol, Donald. *Encyclopedia Brown and the Case of the Slippery Salamander.*
This book is one of the latest in a series of stories about Encyclopedia Brown. You can try to solve each mystery on your own. Then, you can find the solution in the back of the book.

Soto, Gary. *Skirt.* (Contemporary Fiction)
Soto has written many other books, including *Baseball in April and Other Stories* and *Crazy Weekend. Summer on Wheels* is the sequel to *Crazy Weekend.*

Speare, Elizabeth. *The Sign of the Beaver.* (Historical Fiction)
Also try Speare's classic, *The Witch of Blackbird Pond.*

Stolz, Mary. *Go Fish.*

White, E. B. *Charlotte's Web.* (Classic)
Also try White's other books for children: *Stuart Little* and *The Trumpet of the Swan.*

Wilder, Laura Ingalls. *The Little House in the Big Woods.* (Classic, Historical Fiction)
This book is the first in Wilder's series about her life as a pioneer girl. The second book in the series is *Little House on the Prairie.*

Yep, Laurence. *Ribbons.* (Contemporary Fiction)
The Cook's Family is the sequel to this book.

The Princeton Review
State Assessment Services

Parents
Help your child succeed using the same tool teachers use.

Solutions for Virginia Parents

●●● **Homeroom.com:** Assess, analyze, remediate

●●● **Test-Specific Prep Books:** Providing proven strategies